PLAYERS' INTERACTION IN

INTERNATIONAL ARBITRATION

DOSSIERS
ICC INSTITUTE OF WORLD BUSINESS LAW

ICC Services
Publications Department
38 COURS ALBERT 1ER
75008 PARIS
FRANCE

ICC PUBLICATION NO. 737E
ISBN: 978-92-842-0167-9

TABLE OF CONTENTS

FOREWORD..5
YVES DERAINS

INTRODUCTION..7
BERNARD HANOTIAU, CO-EDITOR

CHAPTER ONE..9
WHAT DUTIES DO COUNSEL OWE TO THE TRIBUNAL AND WHY?
HORACIO A. GRIGERA NAÓN

CHAPTER TWO..23
DOCUMENT EXCHANGES AND THE COLLISION OF ETHICAL DUTIES OF COUNSEL FROM DIFFERENT
LEGAL SYSTEMS
DOAK BISHOP AND MARGRETE STEVENS

CHAPTER THREE...35
THE ROLE OF USERS
V.V. VEEDER

CHAPTER FOUR...43
IN-HOUSE COUNSEL: WHY THEY SHOULD BE MORE INVOLVED IN THE ARBITRAL PROCESS
KARL HENNESSEE

CHAPTER FIVE..49
THE TRIBUNAL'S RIGHTS AND DUTIES: WHAT DO PARTIES AND ARBITRATORS BARGAIN FOR?
JULIAN .M. LEW, QC

CHAPTER SIX..67
THE CHAIRMAN'S ROLE IN THE ARBITRAL TRIBUNAL'S DYNAMICS
LAURENT LÉVY

CHAPTER SEVEN...87
SECRETARIES TO ARBITRAL TRIBUNALS
CONSTANTINE PARTASIDES

CHAPTER EIGHT..93
IMMUNITY AND LIABILITY OF ARBITRATORS: WHAT IS THE PROPER BALANCE?
EDUARDO SILVA ROMERO

CHAPTER NINE..99
DO INSTITUTIONS REALLY ADD VALUE TO THE ARBITRAL PROCESS?
KARL-HEINZ BÖCKSTIEGEL

CHAPTER TEN..105
RECIPROCAL DUTIES OF INSTITUTIONS AND ARBITRATORS
PETER LEAVER, QC

CHAPTER ELEVEN..113
TRANSPARENCY: IS IT REALLY NEEDED AND TO WHAT EXTENT?
JUDITH GILL, QC

CHAPTER TWELVE...121
LIABILITY OF ARBITRATION INSTITUTIONS: WHAT DOES THE FUTURE HOLD?
TERESA Y.W CHENG AND JUSTIN LI

CHAPTER THIRTEEN...131
DEBATE:DOES EACH PLAYER MEET THE OTHERS' EXPECTATIONS?
DOES THE ARBITRATION PROCESS MEET THE USERS' EXPECTATIONS?
JEAN-ANDRÉ DIAZ, HAMID GHARAVI, ANNETTE MAGNUSSON, PIERRE TERCIER

CONCLUDING REMARKS..147
ALEXIS MOURRE, CO-EDITOR

INDEX...151

TABLE OF CASES...167

ABOUT THE AUTHORS..169

THE INTERNATIONAL CHAMBER OF COMMERCE...180

SOME ICC SPECIALIZED DIVISIONS..181

ICC PUBLICATION FOR GLOBAL BUSINESS...182

LATEST ARBITRATION PUBLICATION FROM ICC...183

FOREWORD

BY YVES DERAINS
MEMBER OF THE PARIS BAR
CHAIRMAN, ICC INSTITUTE OF WORLD BUSINESS LAW

This ninth Dossier of the Institute focuses on the main participants in the arbitration process: the parties, their lawyers, the arbitrators, their secretaries and the arbitral institutions. Although the above are described illustratively, this Dossier is not an album of photos. Its approach is definitely dynamic. Photos are replaced by film. The word "players" in the title has been chosen on purpose. What particularly interested the speakers and the audience of the 2011 Annual Conference of the Institute is the evolution of the complex and multiple interactions between the participants in an arbitration procedure before, during, and after the proceedings. All the players in an arbitration process are presented in action.

Lawyers like to use movie vocabulary when discussing their performance: were they any good, did they use the right tone, did they overact? Legal briefs often begin with a list of dramatis personae, even if the author may have forgotten that in Latin the word persona originally meant "actor's mask" before it came to signify a "role". There are several reasons for this use of movie analogy. Like a movie, an arbitration process tells a story in this case one which is full of flashbacks. The players in an arbitration procedure have a specific role to play and must respect given rules, much in the same way as people making a movie must. Participants in the hearing impersonate the characters of the President, the arbitrator and the counsel. They stop addressing each other by their first name, and for some hours or days play the role that has been assigned to them. But the analogy between movies and arbitration cannot go very far. Firstly, an arbitration is not a product of the entertainment industry. Not so much because it remains largely confidential, but because it can have very serious repercussions in the real life of one or all of the parties. Secondly, and more significantly, whereas the cast and crew of a movie are supposed to share a common goal–the production of a successful movie–the players in an arbitration procedure do not share the same agenda.

Arbitral institutions are eager to organize a good arbitration which leads to an award enforceable by law. The arbitrators' goal is to achieve justice, both from a procedural and substantive point of view.

However, they also want to manage the case within a reasonable time frame and at reasonable cost, as both these factors are a source of tension. Few lawyers are interested in either the quality of the arbitration or the correctness of the decision taken. Their objective is to win the case or, if they know it is impossible to win, to limit the inevitable loss that their client is going to suffer. At the same time they need to show their clients that they are fighting hard for them in order to maintain their confidence, which can lead to a level of confrontation with the opposing parties and sometimes with the arbitrators, both of which are counterproductive. Finally, there is no common approach among the clients. It depends on their company's position in each case. But, in general, although they expect a fast and economic resolution of the dispute, they also wish to present their case without any limitation, regardless of the length or costs of the procedure. The interaction between those players with different but legitimate interests requires that, beyond the application of the rules of specific arbitration institutions and of some national procedural law, the rules of the game and basic ethical principles must be respected. The major players were very active at the 2011 Annual Conference of the Institute. Their presentations and the following discussions contributed to a better understanding of the need for such rules and principles. The reciprocal rights and duties at stake have been thoroughly analyzed. As a result, this IX Dossier is set to become another great vintage work in the Collection.

INTRODUCTION

The Council of the ICC Institute of World Business Law chose the interaction between actors in international arbitration as the theme for its annual seminar in December 2011.

In recent decades, arbitration has met with growing, even exponential, success. What used to be the business of a few specialized attorneys and a limited number of counsel has become an industry with a plethora of actors. This translates into a growing interest of lawyers in international arbitration, an increase in the number of institutions and, in parallel, the publication year after year of ever more journals—more or less technical—which are accompanied by a proliferation of seminars, trainings, congresses and education daystraining sessions and conferences. We have also witnessed the birth of companies specialized in financing arbitration procedures, namely so-called third-party funders.

Unfortunately, these considerable developments do not only have good sides. Arbitral procedures have seemingly become longer, costlier and more complex, and all actors complain about this.

In recent years, many actors have tended—incorrectly, in my view—to impute such problems too easily to arbitrators. Arbitrators do, of course, bear some responsibility in this regard. However, as law firms specialized in arbitration have become more sophisticated—with the good and bad that this brings—and busier, even overwhelmed, time limits have become longer (and fee notes bigger) and, despite this, procedural calendars are less respected. Institutions are also not far behind. Where several years ago the constitution of an arbitral tribunal or the notification of an award took several days, they can nowadays take several weeks or months. The increasing complexity of arbitral rules and the growth in guidelines and regulations of all kinds are no doubt largely responsible.

It thus seemed to us—like other institutions, for that matter, such as ICCA—that it was time to rethink the arbitral process and to address the interaction between the participants of international arbitration and, in this context, the respective rights and obligations of each, the final goal being to contribute together, as much as possible, to the improvement of the process, while respecting the ultimate goal of dispensing justice in a respectful and efficient manner, within short time limits, without costing too much to the parties to the procedure.

In this context, the council structured its analysis around four themes. The first theme focused on the duties that counsel and parties have towards each other and towards the arbitral tribunal. This theme was dealt with by four speakers. Horacio Grigera Naon addressed the duties of counsel towards the tribunal. Doak Bishop dealt with the question of whether "anything goes" in obtaining evidence. Johnny Veeder, QC, investigated whether counsel and clients really share the same interests.

Finally, Karl Hennessee submitted some thoughts and proposals regarding the need for greater involvement of in-house counsel in the arbitral procedure.

The problems addressed in the context of the second theme focused on the efficient functioning of the arbitral tribunal. First, Professor Julian Lew analyzed the rights and duties of the arbitral tribunal. Laurent Lévy then addressed more specifically the role of the chairman of the arbitral tribunal in its internal dynamics. In addition, since arbitrators' use of administrative secretaries is becoming increasingly common, Constantine Partasides attempted to identify good practices in this respect. Finally, Eduardo Silva Romero investigated the liability and immunity of arbitrators and tried to define the right balance between these two concepts.

The third session focused on the role of institutions. The question whether they truly add value to the procedure was dealt with by Professor Karl-Heinz Böckstiegel. Peter Leaver then spoke about the mutual rights and duties of institutions and arbitrators. Finally, Judith Gill, QC, examined the extent to which institutions must ensure procedural transparency, and Teresa Cheng considered the question of their liability.

The last session was devoted to a general debate on whether the various actors in international arbitration meet the expectations of the other participants and whether users are satisfied with the arbitral procedure. In this context, a representative of each group was invited to present a position: for in-house counsel, Jean-André Diaz; for counsel, Hamid Gharavi; for the institutions, Annette Magnusson; and, finally, for the arbitrators, Professor Pierre Tercier.

In keeping with the tradition of previous years, the Council of the ICC Institute of World Business Law has sought to ensure the publication of the papers presented at the seminar. The council hopes that the thoughts, suggestions and proposals formulated over the course of this seminar will be of great use to the arbitration community in its process of reconsidering the role of—and interaction between—the different participants in the arbitral procedure. Likewise, we hope that they will contribute to achieving the final goal of ensuring the harmonious and efficient functioning of the arbitration process in terms of time and cost, while respecting the legitimate expectations of the parties.

Bernard Hanotiau

CHAPTER ONE

WHAT DUTIES DO COUNSEL OWE TO THE TRIBUNAL AND WHY?

Horacio A. Grigera Naón

1. INTRODUCTION

It is perhaps trite—but not without importance—to state that the main objective of an international commercial arbitration procedure is to ensure the fair and efficient handling and resolution of international commercial disputes.

Attaining this objective requires not only the provision of a satisfactory and reliable service to the parties involved but also the meeting of certain systemic expectations of the general public—potential arbitration users—in order to maintain its respect. Arbitrators have an interest in attaining this objective not only because of the detrimental effect on the parties of failing to provide such a service but also because their reputation and the reputation of international commercial arbitration as the best method for the settlement of international commercial disputes would certainly suffer if they fail to meet certain expectations.

An important part of these expectations—both systemic and those of the parties to the arbitration—is that certain standards of mutual respect, loyalty, courtesy, integrity, dignity, good faith conduct and professionalism are observed by counsel in their interaction with the arbitral tribunal (the "tribunal"), since an arbitration can best be carried out efficiently and in an orderly manner when counsel act in good faith and with a cooperative spirit within the context of the appropriate procedural surroundings.

Living up to such standards is an essential part of the duties owed by counsel to the tribunal as the guardian of the efficient and fair management and conduct of the arbitration and the preservation of its integrity. In fact, the duties of counsel regarding the efficiency and integrity of the arbitral proceedings are duties not only to the tribunal but also to the opposing counsel and party, which are equally entitled to an efficient and fair arbitration. It is also possible that counsel who do not properly fulfil these duties would consequently also fail to fulfil their duties vis-à-vis the appointing party, since their misconduct could adversely affect the tribunal's vision of their client's case. In certain situations, it would therefore be artificial to attempt to make a clear distinction among or isolate such duties.

In performing such duties, however, counsel have to strike a balance between the duties owed to the tribunal and the specific duty of advancing the case of the party they represent. Ethical rules governing lawyers' conduct partly reflect the need to strike such a balance. For example, article 4.3 (Demeanour in Court) of the Code of Conduct for Lawyers in the European Union approved by the Council of the Bars and Law Societies of the European Union[1] provides that:

> *"A lawyer shall while maintaining due respect and courtesy towards the court defend the interests of his client honourably and fearlessly without regard to his own interests or to any consequences to himself or any other person."*[2]

The Code further provides that counsel "must always have due regard to the conduct of the proceedings" and "not make contact with the judge without first informing the lawyer acting for the opposing party" (article 4.2). Article 4.4 of the Code provides: "A lawyer shall never knowingly give false or misleading information to the court."

Although not specifically intended to apply to lawyering in international commercial arbitrations, another example of such rules appears in the International Bar Association's International Code of Ethics.[3]

Reference may be also made to the more recent IBA General Principles for the Legal Profession,[4] which provides in Principle 2 (Honesty, integrity and fairness):

> *"A lawyer shall at all times maintain the highest standards of honesty, integrity and fairness towards the Court, his or her colleagues and all those with whom he or she comes professionally into contact."*

Furthermore, Principle 5 (Clients' interest) provides:

> *"A lawyer shall treat the interests of his or her clients as paramount, subject always to his or her duties to the Court and the interests of justice, to observe the law and to maintain ethical standards."*

In the official Commentary,[5] the term Court or tribunal used in the Principles is defined as including "an arbitrator in a binding arbitration proceeding".

A more specific statement of counsel's duties in arbitration and the balance to be struck in fulfilling them was made in a recent arbitral decision:[6]

> *"Counsel's duty is to present his Party's case, with the degree of dependence and partiality that the role implies, so long as he does so with diligence and with honesty, and in due compliance with the applicable rules of professional conduct and ethics."*

2. FAILURE OF COUNSEL TO EXHIBIT PROPER CONDUCT

Experience generally proves that counsel exhibit courteous and respectful conduct in respect of the tribunal, although the interaction between counsel of the parties to an arbitration does not always display the same civility.

However, courtesy is only one of the standards of conduct to be met by counsel in regard to the tribunal and the efficiency and integrity of the arbitral procedure. In addition, the above-mentioned standards are couched in language that is too open-ended, lack sufficient substance to be useful[7] or do not specifically cover matters arising in international commercial arbitration scenarios because they generally address counsel conduct before national courts.

For example, ethical codes do not capture in sufficient detail counsel's duties towards the tribunal in connection with the efficiency and fairness of the arbitral procedure, such as avoiding unnecessarily time-consuming conduct, reducing costs often associated with delays or the ill-use of time and maximizing the ratio of material information and evidence presented to the arbitrators over information or evidence that is immaterial or irrelevant.[8] Moreover, counsel's duties in regard to the integrity of the arbitral proceedings, which the tribunal is obliged to safeguard, also need to be specifically considered and addressed.

Real problems arise when counsel exhibit procedural conduct that negatively affects the efficiency of the arbitration, thus failing to properly comply with their duties either:

(a) because of a lack of experience in international commercial arbitration or a lack of adequate preparation, including a lack of thorough knowledge of the case in question; or

(b) because counsel are advancing procedural strategies that are specifically aimed at—or, if not intentionally aimed at, in any case have the practical effect of—advantaging their case and disadvantaging the case of their opponents, with the effect of introducing delays or disruptions into the swift conduct of the arbitral proceedings.

a. Lack of experience and/or preparation

International arbitration counsel have the professional duty to be properly equipped and trained in the area of international commercial arbitration, for example to free themselves from the influence of parochial procedural concepts ill-adapted to in-ternational arbitration cases, as well as the professional duty to properly prepare their case. Although problems in both areas are probably on the wane because counsel are increasingly well informed about their expected role in international commercial arbitration and increasingly well prepared to deal with international arbitration cases, the following are some real life scenarios intended to illustrate the above-mentioned problems.

The first one concerns an ICC international arbitration that was conducted in Span-ish and whose seat was located in a Latin American country. Because counsel to both parties, which were nationals of this country, insisted on handling the arbitra-tion as they would a local court litigation, they requested of the tribunal that:

(1)   all questions to the witnesses and experts, including questions coming from opposing counsel, be submitted in writing to the chairman of the tribunal, who would then put the question to the expert or fact witness, with only the chairman having the ability to reformulate or not formulate such questions if he or she considered them to be improper or inadequate;

(2)   both counsel refused to provide written statements for fact witnesses and only accepted to present in advance short summaries of the matters to be covered by witness testimony; and

(3)   in addition to the party-appointed experts, the tribunal would have its own expert, who would issue his or her own separate expert report after considering the expert reports of the party-appointed experts. After the submission of the third expert's report, the parties' experts and their counsel would be afforded the opportunity to comment on the third expert's report.

Obviously, the technique for questioning witnesses pushed by counsel is far removed from international arbitration practices, according to which cross-examination carried out by opposing counsel plays an important role in the understanding of the case by the arbitrators. However, the tribunal was confronted with a difficult situation, not only because counsel for both parties had agreed on the above procedures and did not wish to depart from them but also because it became clear that they lacked cross-examination skills. The tribunal's chairman and the other members of the tribunal were thus forced to attempt to overcome this deficiency by formulating questions on their own initiative. This was not ideal, since their knowledge of the parties' respective cases most likely did not match the parties' counsel's own knowledge and ensuing ability to examine the witnesses.

After looking into the facts of the case and the expert witness reports submitted by the parties' experts, the tribunal was of the view that the appointment of the third expert was not needed. However, the tribunal had to give in to the firm request of both counsel to appoint the third expert, which, in addition to an unnecessary increase in arbitral costs and loss of time, in any case brought about the following negative effects:

(1)   Potential candidates had to be selected from a pool of local experts with experience in an industry with few local experts and players. For these reasons, it was very difficult to find an expert who was independent of both parties.

(2)   It was not easy to have the parties agree on the expert's remuneration.

(3)   The third expert's testimony turned out to be useless, since it did not add much to the opinions of the other experts or throw significant light on the matters on which the latter did not coincide. Part of the problem seemed to be that, prompted by *esprit de corps*, the third expert avoided saying anything that conflicted radically with the other experts' opinions.

The need for the tribunal to deal with the above matters and the absence of counsel's predisposition to depart from their rigid and pre-conceived ideas on how to structure an international commercial arbitral procedure significantly conspired against both the efficient management of the case and its understanding by the arbitrators, and added unnecessary complications to the conduct of the arbitration.

The second example, which I have seen in both ICC and ICDR arbitrations, is the insistence by counsel in international cases on adhering to forms of production of evidence (US style discovery) that are clearly inappropriate for international commercial arbitration.

This may happen, for example, if both counsel agree on US style discovery (e.g., by expressly indicating that the US Federal Rules of Procedure shall apply), despite the tribunal's suggestions to the contrary. In extreme cases, this may involve not only a full disclosure of documents at the beginning of the case but also the use of admissions, interrogatories, depositions and aggressive applications for the production of documents from the opposing party. Not infrequently, counsel also agree on having live direct testimony without written witness statements in lieu of direct examination, which leads to protracted hearings, sometimes lasting several weeks, with the accompanying increase in the costs and time devoted to the case. Such evidentiary tools, designed to present cases before juries—that is to say, inexperienced triers of fact that often lack legal training and/or have never (or only occasionally) been confronted with the task of deciding disputes—are ill-adapted to pleading a case before legally trained and experienced arbitrators.

In such situations, the tribunal may have to issue directions aimed at somewhat attenuating the use of discovery, such as limiting the number of depositions and their length, defining with precision their role and providing for a tight schedule for interrogatories, admissions and the deposition exercise. For example, rather than using depositions to highlight contradictions between the live testimony of the witness before the tribunal and his or her deposition, the tribunal can limit their purpose to identifying additional evidence not so far produced through information gathered during the deposition, while retaining discretion to call the party or witness making the deposition for live testimony to the hearing. However, such efforts by the tribunal only partially succeed in reducing the adverse impact on the efficient management of the case brought about by the above-mentioned counsel-imposed discovery practices.

In this context, moreover, counsel not infrequently insist on being allowed to request the production of documents under the control of the opposing party on a rolling basis. As a result, the tribunal is often called to decide document production disputes and to repeatedly use its discretion to reasonably moderate requests for the disclosure of documents in order to prevent this exercise from becoming an unduly oppressive, time-consuming and expensive burden on the party to which the request is addressed.

b. Counsel strategy and tactics

Situations falling under this category may turn out to be more problematic, since they often directly concern counsel's duty to advocate in good faith and without harming the integrity of arbitral proceedings. Such situations particularly require counsel, in fulfilment of their duties, to strike a proper balance between their obligation to advance the interests of their client and their obligation to contribute to having efficient arbitral proceedings that are fair to all parties involved in the dispute. In extreme scenarios, rather than as a consequence of lack of experience, failure to strike such a balance may be the result of a specific counsel strategy that involves inappropriate conduct or even misconduct.

Such problems may present themselves in different scenarios, some of which will be considered below.

The first tactic may consist of intentionally abusive or aggressive unilateral applications by counsel of one of the parties for the production of documents under the control of the opposing party more aligned with US-style discovery.

This tactic is not infrequently pursued by non-US lawyers, with the aggravation that, unlike US lawyers, they seem unaware of the limitations that, within a US setting, attenuate or exclude US discovery tactics in arbitration, domestic or otherwise,[9] as well as those prevailing in international arbitral practice.[10]

This tactic becomes particularly disruptive when, due to a lack of cooperation, counsel do not meet and confer to resolve differences arising from evidentiary matters, including document production, which would normally exclude or substantially minimize the need to involve the tribunal in the resolution of such differences. Failure to do so translates into repeated applications to the tribunal to decide on such differences, sometimes requiring the consideration by the tribunal of privilege and confidentiality issues. This has a negative impact on the efficient conduct of the arbitration, although in many instances those differences could have been more expeditiously and effectively resolved, or at least reasonably reduced, through counsel's direct cooperative efforts.[11]

Other tactics consist of repeatedly raising objections to the questioning of witnesses, which may require an answer from opposing counsel and/or a determination of the tribunal. One way of dealing with such conduct—which in itself disrupts the hearing—is just to take note of the objection when manifestly unjustified and invite opposing counsel to continue with the questioning of the witness. It may be helpful, in connection with certain types of objections and in order to avoid their repetition, for the tribunal to clarify certain matters, such as the admissibility in international arbitration of hearsay evidence and—within certain limits—leading questions. However, other objections may be part of a sandbagging strategy aimed at laying traps to be used in a future attempt to challenge the arbitral award or the arbitrators. In such cases, objections need to be fully ventilated and decided during the hearing or before it comes to an end, even if this results in a loss of time and a deterioration in the cooperative atmosphere that should ideally be present throughout the hearing.

But perhaps the more problematic situations, which strain the conduct of the arbitral proceedings and the interactions of those involved in it, come about when certain issues are raised in the course of the arbitration that cast doubts on the integrity of counsel and—potentially—on the integrity of the arbitral proceedings. Such situations are particularly delicate, since they require the tribunal to find a prudent balance between the right of a party to choose its own counsel and the right of counsel, as part of their duty to render proper services to their client, to incorporate into the counsel's team those who are best equipped to present and defend the client's case, on the one hand, and the counsel's duty to contribute to the integrity of the arbitral proceedings, on the other.

Not infrequently, such situations lead to delays and even disruptions in the efficient handling of arbitral proceedings, since they require the elucidation of difficult issues, such as whether counsel has been involved in the spoliation of evidence, like the destruction of documents or electronic data, or identifying the rules or requirements applying to the preservation of documents and data that may later prove relevant in arbitration or litigation.[12] They often also require several rounds of written submissions or evidence, including the presentation of expert evidence, the consideration of complex matters, including choice-of-law matters,[13] and the adoption of partial decisions or awards not dealing with, delaying a decision on or distracting efforts that would otherwise be applied to deciding the merits of the case. They may lead to strained interactions between parties or their counsel, and also have the potential to create otherwise avoidable complications in the management of the case by the tribunal. Such situations may concern conduct that, in principle, is attributable to counsel, the party they represent or both, with the accompanying difficulty of discerning who is responsible and who is not.

Finally, such situations not only raise issues concerning the fulfilment of counsel's duties in respect of the integrity of the arbitral proceedings and the tribunal's duty of guarding this integrity but also make it necessary to define the authority and jurisdiction of the tribunal in order to determine matters such as the exclusion of counsel from the arbitration.

Two ICC arbitrations may be mentioned in this connection.

c. Examples

The first arbitration[14] concerned a law firm that, prior to the initiation of arbitral proceedings, had given advice to the claimant regarding a comapny that later became the respondent in arbitration proceedings between the two parties. As part of this advice, the law firm issued an opinion that found the future respondent's by-laws to be valid under the applicable law. After the initiation of arbitral proceedings, the same law firm appeared as counsel for the respondent and raised as one of the defences against the claimant's claims the invalidity of the respondent's by-laws.

The second arbitration—a construction case—concerned sanctions requested in an ICC arbitration against the claimant and its counsel because of the incorporation into the joint bundle prepared for a hearing on the merits of internal documents from the opposing party that were allegedly confidential or subject to privilege and had allegedly been obtained by the claimant outside of the document production process and from sources unknown. Such documents had apparently been received through electronic means or in the form of a hard copy anonymously delivered to officers of the claimant. An initial search of back-up tapes and metadata did not result in an unequivocal conclusion regarding the source of the documents conveyed by electronic means. The source of the hard-copy documents could not be identified either.

In addition to delicate issues affecting the integrity of the arbitral proceedings, one of the difficulties common to both situations is the applicable law or rules to be observed by the arbitrators. Such law or rules define both the arbitral jurisdiction to discipline counsel misconduct and the arbitrators' duties in this regard. So far, there does not seem to be a unified approach to these issues.

In the first case, the arbitrators held that the matters before them involved the consideration of criminal conduct or the application of sanctions under national law or national bar disciplinary rules for inappropriate or illicit counsel conduct and that the responsibility for the enforcement of those sanctions did not lie with the arbitrators but with the national courts or bar authority. Furthermore, the arbitrators concluded that the issue in question fell outside their jurisdiction and that excluding counsel would go against the fundamental principle that parties are entitled to the counsel of their choice. In the end, no sanctions were imposed, and counsel were not excluded from the case.

In the second case, the potentially applicable laws or rules included the laws or disciplinary rules of the bar authority corresponding to the jurisdiction in which the counsel accused of improper or illicit conduct was registered and the laws and ethical or disciplinary rules of the seat of the arbitration. As in the previous case, the tribunal concluded that it was not its role to enforce such rules or laws. However, the tribunal stated that it was its obligation to protect the integrity of the arbitral proceedings in accordance with standards of fairness and due process, laid down in article 15(2) of the—then applicable—ICC Arbitration Rules, and at the same time to respect the public policy principles (in the sense of *ordre public international*) underlying the laws of the seat of the arbitration aimed at protecting the integrity of the arbitration process.

The tribunal also noted that one of the paramount objectives of the law of the seat was precisely to safeguard the integrity and fairness of the arbitral procedure and that, under the law of the seat, the sanctions for improper conduct damaging these protected values included disqualification of counsel, dismissal of the claims of the party responsible for the inappropriate or bad-faith conduct, and exclusion of the evidence obtained through improper means. Both parties accepted that such sanctions could come into play if the existence of such conduct were verified.

The tribunal found that there was no body of universally accepted principles in the area of international commercial arbitration to deal with such issues except for the obligation of the tribunal to ensure that the arbitral procedure be carried out in a fair way that allowed all parties to be sufficiently heard.[15] The tribunal also held that this obligation, an essential part of the mission entrusted to it, entitled the tribunal to assert jurisdiction on the matters that—like those before it—directly concerned the integrity of the arbitral proceedings. However, the tribunal made clear that such standards were not to be evaluated in the abstract but had to be applied against the backdrop of the specific expectations and conduct of the parties in question and previous rulings of the tribunal on document production.

Although the tribunal was of the view that the mere fact of obtaining documentary evidence under the control of the opposing party outside of the document production process pursuant to the procedural orders issued by the tribunal was not *per se* irregular or illegal, it found that the relevant standards included the obligation of a party to inform the opposing party about the receipt of documents outside of the discovery process and that could be considered as privileged as soon as they were identified, to cease further review or use of such documents, and to exclude from the proceedings documents in respect of which there was a valid assertion of privilege or confidentiality. The tribunal's final conclusion was to exclude from the evidence most of the documents obtained outside of the normal production process without imposing sanctions on the claimant or its counsel.[16]

The problem presents itself in a different dimension when the conduct of counsel may have a bearing on the appearance of impartiality of the tribunal in discharging its duties. Such a situation was the subject of the decisions of two ICSID tribunals in *Hrvatska Elektroprivreda d.d. v. The Republic of Slovenia* (hereinafter, the Hrvatska case)[17] and *The Rompetrol Group N.V. v. Romania* (hereinafter, the Rompetrol case).[18]

The issue in the *Hrvatska case* was whether English counsel belonging to the same chambers as the chairman of the tribunal, who had been incorporated into the respondent's counsel team shortly before the hearing and had attended the hearing without first disclosing this relationship, should be allowed to participate in the case. In the *Rompetrol case*, the issue was the replacement of the lead counsel in charge of the case on behalf of the claimant with a professional who had recently been a member of the same law firm to which the arbitrator appointed by the claimant belonged. In neither of these instances did the opposing party seek the removal of the chairman of the tribunal or the claimant's arbitrator, as the case may be. In the *Hrvatska case*, the tribunal excluded the controversial counsel from the proceedings; in the *Rompetrol case*, it did not.

Without entering into the factual differences between both cases, which in part account for the different outcome,[19] it is worth comparing the rationale followed by the respective tribunals in reaching their conclusion.

In the *Hrvatska case*, the tribunal first noted that the ICSID Convention and Arbitration Rules do not expressly vest arbitrators with the authority to exclude counsel and that the general principle was the freedom of parties to select the counsel of their choice.[20] However, it also pointed out that this principle was subject to exceptions when other overriding principles are at stake, such as the immutability of ICSID tribunals once properly constituted,[21] which could not be negatively affected by the supervening circumstance created by adding a lawyer to the respondent's counsel team. Another fundamental principle accounting for the tribunal's jurisdiction to decide in favour of the exclusion of counsel[22] is the tribunal's obligation and inherent power to preserve the integrity of the proceedings and its award under international law and the ICSID Convention,[23] which would be tainted if any justified doubt as to the impartiality or independence of any member of the tribunal could exist in the eyes of a reasonable and independent observer. The tribunal concluded that such circumstances were present in the case at hand.[24]

In the *Rompetrol case*, the tribunal was certainly more doubtful as to its power to exclude counsel.[25] Although apparently ready to accept it in exceptional circumstances, the carefully chosen and cautious wording in the decision dealing with this issue evidences the reluctance of the *Rompetrol* tribunal to fully endorse the *Hrvatska* tribunal's approach.[26]

Be that as it may, it is plausible, as highlighted by the *Rompetrol* tribunal,[27] that a different perception in the *Hrvatska case* of how claimant's counsel's duties in respect of the fairness of the arbitral proceedings (and towards the arbitral tribunal as guardian of such fairness) had been fulfilled was determinative for the different outcome in both cases. In other words, the balance struck by counsel between their perception of their duties towards the party appointing them, on the one hand, and the duties towards the arbitral procedure and the tribunal regarding the integrity of the arbitration, on the other, was judged to be inappropriate by the *Hrvatska* tribunal and to be appropriate by the *Rompetrol* tribunal.

It is also worth mentioning that, in apparently similar but in fact quite different situations, appointing counsel that have or had a significant professional connection to one of the members of the tribunal during the course of the arbitral proceedings may be a bad faith tactic designed to create grounds for challenging the tribunal member by showing this connection to be in violation of counsel's good faith duties towards the integrity of the proceedings and the arbitrators. Of course, this was not the case in the *Hrvatska case* or the *Rompetrol case*, in which no removal of an arbitrator was sought. In the particular context of the Rompetrol case, there is no reason to believe that the claimant was seeking to create grounds to remove its own appointed arbitrator.

3. CONCLUSION

The different situations considered in this paper are exceptional and no attempt is made to present an unrealistically gloomy picture or cast an unnecessarily negative shadow on the large majority of able and honest practitioners composing the international arbitral bar.[28]

The fact that such situations are not the general rule makes one wonder if it is really necessary, as an increasingly copious literature suggests, to create a more specific body of international ethical rules for arbitral counsel not only with regard to their relationship to the tribunal but also in respect of all those involved in international commercial arbitrations. To legislate or provide abstract guidelines in the absence of a concrete and pressing need and substantial experience gleaned from international commercial arbitration practice addressing such situations may prove counterproductive, not least because of the difficulty of dealing through general rules or guidelines with an often unpredictable combination of circumstances and issues that often defies the imagination.

It may well be that it would be better, for the time being, to allow tribunals to address such situations as they present themselves on a case-by-case basis. In any event, this is not a matter to be left to conjecture or an abstract comparison of national legal systems or local bar regulations governing the conduct of lawyers. Prior to issuing rules or guidelines, a field study of actual international commercial arbitration practice, necessarily including consultations with practitioners, arbitrators and other players with proven experience in this area of the law, appears to be in order.[29] However, like other questions in the always-challenging field of international commercial arbitration, this is open to debate.

ENDNOTES:

1   Adopted at the CCBE Plenary Session held on 28 October 1988, and subsequently amended during the CCBE Plenary Sessions on 28 November 1998 and 6 December 2002. Articles 1.4 and 1.5 of the Code limit its application to lawyers of the European Union and the European Economic Area and, *ratione materiae*, to professional contacts among member states' lawyers or to the activities of a lawyer in a member state other than his or her own.

2   According to article 4.5 of this Code: "The rules governing a lawyer's relations with the courts apply also to his relations with arbitrators and any other persons exercising judicial or quasi-judicial functions, even on occasional basis."

3   First adopted in 1956, last amended in 1988. According to Rule 6: "Lawyers shall always maintain due respect towards the Court. Lawyers shall without fear defend the interests of their clients and without regard to any unpleasant consequences to themselves or any other person. Lawyers shall never knowingly give to the Court incorrect information or advice which is to their knowledge contrary to the law." Rule 1 provides: "A lawyer who undertakes professional work in a jurisdiction where he is not a full member of the local profession shall adhere to the standards of professional ethics in the jurisdiction in which he has been admitted. He shall also observe all ethical standards which apply to lawyers of the country where he is working."

4   Adopted by the International Bar Association on 20 September 2006.

5   Adopted by the International Bar Association at the Warsaw Council Meeting on 28 May 2011.

6   ICSID case no. ARB/06/3 *The Rompetrol Group N.V. v. Romania*, at para. 19.

7   V.V. Veeder, 'The 2001 Goff Lecture—The Lawyer's Duty to Arbitrate in Good Faith', *Arbitration International* 18 (2002) p. 431.

8   C. Clarke, 'Missed Manners in Court Room Decorum', *Maryland Law Review* 50 (1991) p. 945.

9   For example, section 17(c) of the US Uniform Arbitration Act provides: "An arbitrator may permit such discovery as the arbitrator decides is appropriate in the circumstances, taking into account the needs of the parties to the arbitration proceeding and other affected persons and the desirability of making the proceeding fair, expeditious, and cost effective." The official comment on this provision states: "Most commentators and courts conclude that extensive discovery, as allowed in civil litigation, eliminates the main advantages of arbitration in terms of cost, speed and efficiency. ... At the same time, it should be clear that in many arbitrations discovery is unnecessary and that discovery contemplated by Section 17(c) ... is not coextensive with that which occurs in the course of civil litigation under federal rules or state rules of civil procedure. Although Section 17 (c) allows an arbitrator to permit discovery so that parties can obtain necessary information, the intent of the language is to limit discovery by considerations of fairness, efficiency and cost."

In a similar vein, article 1(a) of the ICDR Guidelines for Arbitrators Concerning Exchanges of Information provides: "The tribunal shall manage the exchange of information in advance of the hearings with a view to maintaining efficiency and economy. The tribunal and the parties should endeavor to avoid unnecessary delay and expense while at the same time balancing the goals of avoiding surprise, promoting equality of treatment, and safeguarding each party's opportunity to present its claims and defenses fairly." Article 6(a) further provides: "Arbitrators should be receptive to creative solutions for achieving exchanges of information in ways that avoid costs and delay, consistent with the principles of due process expressed in these Guidelines." In addition, article 6(b) provides: "Depositions, interrogatories, and requests to admit, as developed in American court procedures, are generally not appropriate procedures for obtaining information in international arbitration."

10   For example, article 3(3) (defining the contents of a request to produce documents) and article 9(2)(c) (exclusion from the evidence of documents the production of which would be unreasonably burdensome) of the IBA Rules on the Taking of Evidence in International Arbitration (2010).

11   The above should not prevent the tribunal, on the application of counsel or on its own initiative, from exceptionally allowing depositions in international arbitration proceedings in specific situations in which a deposition may help to avoid unnecessary costs and loss of time. This recently happened in an ICC arbitration in which the deposition of a witness in his country of origin was provided for by the tribunal. The deposition took place exclusively in the presence of counsel for both parties and a court reporter and served the purpose of testing the search for documents that the witness had carried out in his capacity as an officer of one of the parties in response to an order for the production of documents addressed to said party. It should be noted that the tribunal reserved the right to call the witness to testify before it if it deemed this was necessary (but this was ultimately not the case).

12   S. Hammond, 'Spoliation in International Arbitration: Is It Time to Reconsider the "Dirty Wars" of the International Arbitral Process?', *Dispute Resolution International* 3 (2009) p. 5.

13   Including double deontology issues. See, for example, paragraphs 1.3 and 2.3 (among others) of the above-mentioned Commentary on the IBA International Principles of Conduct for the Legal Profession.

14   Reported and commented upon in H. Grigera Naón, 'Choice-of-Law Problems in International Commercial Arbitration', *Hague Academy of International Law: Collected Courses 289* (2001) pp. 157-161.

15   As provided for in article 15(2) of the 1998 ICC Arbitration Rules and article 22(4) of the 2012 ICC Arbitration Rules.

16   One of the many delicate issues confronted by the tribunal in this case was how much time and effort was to be devoted in the arbitral procedure to investigating whether actual counsel or party misconduct had taken place, at the risk of seriously delaying and perhaps derailing the normal course of the arbitration, whose primary objective should be to decide the case on the merits. The tribunal put certain limits on how far the investigation exercise could go by indicating that its functions did not include the public function of protecting the administration of justice and the duty to investigate and ultimately punish conduct prejudicial to the integrity of judicial proceedings. Instead, the tribunal's sole purpose was to safeguard the integrity of the arbitration and the equality of the parties and make a decision on the basis of an adequate arbitral record. This suggests that one of the considerations of the tribunal was not to get involved in an inquisitorial exercise that would substantially delay its decision on the merits of the case.

17   ICSID case no. ARB/05/24, Ruling of 6 May 2008.

18   ICSID case no. ARB/06/3, Decision of 14 January 2010.

19   Highlighted in the *Rompetrol case*, para. 25.

20   *Hrvatska case*, para. 24.

21   ICSID Convention, article 56(1). *Hrvatska case*, para. 25.

22   The tribunal strongly asserted its jurisdiction to decide on the issue before it: "The Tribunal disagrees with the contention of Respondent that it has no inherent powers in this regard. It considers that as a judicial formation governed by public international law, the Tribunal has inherent powers to take measures to preserve the integrity of the proceedings. In part, that inherent power finds a textual foothold in Article 44 of the Convention, which authorizes the Tribunal to decide 'any questions of procedure' not expressly dealt with in the Convention,

the ICSID arbitration rules or 'any rule agreed by the parties.' More broadly, there is an 'inherent power of an international court to deal with any issues necessary for the conduct of matters falling within its jurisdiction;' that power 'exists independently of any statutory reference.' In the specific circumstances of the case, it is in the Tribunal's view both necessary and appropriate to take action under its inherent power." (Hrvatska case, para. 33, footnotes omitted)

23   ICSID Convention, article 52(1)(d).

24   *Hrvatska case*, para. 30.

25   *Rompetrol* case, para. 15: "The Hrvatska decision is not of course a binding precedent. The Tribunal observes simply that, if it indeed be correct to attribute to an ICSID Tribunal the powers implied by the *Hrvatska* Tribunal, they would remain powers to be exercised only in extraordinary circumstances, these being circumstances which genuinely touch on the integrity of the arbitral process as assessed by the Tribunal itself…". The tribunal also placed great emphasis on article 6(3) of the European Convention on Human Rights, including among an individual's basic rights the right to "defend himself in person or through legal assistance of his own choosing", although referring to criminal proceedings (at para. 20).

26   Rompetrol case, para. 16: "… One would normally expect to see such a power specifically provided for in the legal texts governing the tribunal and its operation. Absent express provision, the only justification for the tribunal to award itself the power by extrapolation would be an overriding and undeniable need to safeguard the essential integrity of the entire arbitral process. It plainly follows that a control of that kind would fall to be exercised rarely, and then only in compelling circumstances."

27   *Rompetrol case*, para. 25: "… What is however plain beyond a shadow of doubt is that the *Hrvatska* Tribunal was influenced to a material degree by the late announcement of the new appointment as counsel, coupled with the light that had been cast on the surrounding circumstances by the adamant refusal of the appointing Party's representatives to make any disclosure until the very last minute—which they themselves acknowledged before the Tribunal had been an error of judgment. Viewed from this perspective the *Hrvatska* Decision might better be seen as an *ad hoc* sanction for the failure to make proper disclosure in good time than as a holding of more general scope."

28   Counsel that indeed fits the ideal pattern of being "… nimble adapter(s) … ready to try every case in an entirely new way depending on rules of play and the identity and predilections of the decision makers. He or she embraces the challenge of contending with laws and rules, customs and manners that are not his or her own, and is able to appear equally comfortable before any arbitrator in any hearing room in any region of the world". See Y. Fortier and S. Drymer, 'Advocacy from the Arbitrator's Perspective', in D. Bishop and E. Kehoe (eds.), *The Art of Advocacy in International Arbitration* (2010) p. 611.

29   This would require "[s]ystemic cooperation that involves all relevant actors—parties, counsel, arbitrators, arbitral institutions, and national and international regulatory authorities—… to not only developing the content of the new ethical rules, but to implement them and ensure their meaningful enforcement". See K. Rogers, 'The Ethics of Advocacy in International Arbitration', in D. Bishop and E. Kehoe (eds.), *The Art of Advocacy in International Arbitration* (2010) p. 66.

CHAPTER TWO

DOCUMENT EXCHANGES AND THE COLLISION OF ETHICAL DUTIES OF COUNSEL FROM DIFFERENT LEGAL SYSTEMS

Doak Bishop and Margrete Stevens

1. INTRODUCTION

In 2006, the ICC published a Special Supplement on Document Production in International Arbitration in its Bulletin series.[1] The purpose of the Special Supplement was to provide information on document production practices in arbitration in different parts of the world, as compared with court practices, and to suggest ways of "overcoming the unwieldiness of document production" in international commercial arbitration.[2] The contributions covered several European jurisdictions, the United States, Latin America, the Middle East and Singapore. As highlighted in the concluding observations of the Special Supplement, all contributors pointed to the frequently agreed upon fact that "lawyers and arbitrators are generally influenced by their own national background".[3] Some commentators noted that:

> *"[w]here counsel for one or more of the parties is experienced in United States litigation, it is likely that such counsel will seek document discovery. Similarly, United States arbitrators may be more receptive to requests for document production. The nationality as well as the legal training and experience of the participants in an international arbitration may have a significant impact on the extent of document production in the case."[4]*

Elsewhere it was noted that "arbitrations and counsel often bring the 'bag and baggage' of their respective legal cultures, as well as their own timetables, into the process of bridging gaps between practices routed in national procedural traditions".[5]

One contributor emphasized that there had to date been only little experience with respect to discovery in international arbitration proceedings in his part of the world, namely the Middle East,[6] while another contributor referred to the "insecurity" to which lack of familiarity with international arbitration on the part of counsel leads, highlighting that the so-called uneven playing field is not only created by the common law-civil law divide.[7]

In contrasting the rules of international arbitration with local court procedures, one contributor observed that "breaches for document production in international arbitration are subject to less severe sanctions than in court proceedings".[8] By way of example, the contributor observed that "a solicitor acting for a party in an arbitration faces no sanction if he fails to inform his client of the latter's obligations under an order for document production, as an arbitral tribunal has no power to punish the solicitor".[9] Another contributor made reference to the fact that in international arbitration there is no general obligation upon any party to disclose specific documentation that either support its opponent's case or detracts from its own case.[10]

Acknowledging that this approach, in some cases, is the only way in which justice can be reached, a procedural order might be called for that would require each party's legal representative to certify that, to the best of that party's knowledge, after reasonable search, no document remained undisclosed that either supported its opponent's case or detracted from its own case.[11] The commentator noted, however, that such an order could potentially raise quite difficult issues regarding the different ethical rules to which legal representatives from different jurisdictions are subjected.[12]

The *ICC Bulletin* contributions that recorded the views on document production of some of the most eminent practitioners in the area of international arbitration pointed to issues concerning ethical behaviour by counsel but did not discuss these matters in any detail. Yet, the issue of counsel conduct has increasingly come under scrutiny and merits further examination, including in the context of document exchanges.

2. COUNSEL CONDUCT AND ETHICAL ISSUES IN INTERNATIONAL ARBITRATION

In recent years, a number of commentators have advocated that there is a need to establish ethical standards for counsel appearing in international arbitration proceedings.[13] The basic argument for the call for ethical standards comes from concerns regarding the uneven playing field that different national ethics rules can create. The discussion has for the most part focused on conceptual issues, and little progress has been made in the formulation of applicable rules or guidelines.[14] The complexity of the problem is underscored by the fact that commentators hold different views as to the form in which such standards should be articulated. Some have called for binding rules with broad application; others have suggested that individual institutions ought to lead the way; and other proposals have put forward the idea that parties to individual proceedings work through an "ethical checklist" that could be used at the beginning of a case to ensure that the parties, their counsel and the tribunal would be following the same guidelines insofar as ethical standards are concerned.[15] Such a checklist, according to the proposal, would indentify the areas in which ethical standards among counsel might differ and give parties suggested solutions that could be agreed, failing which the tribunal could determine the issues. The proposal that parties' counsel and the tribunal at the outset agree to identify and decide areas of differing ethical rules and obligations is consistent with the observation of another commentator. Noting that the system of international arbitration is essentially self-policing and recalling that fairness can be harmed by the conduct of the parties' legal representatives, this commentator concluded that self-policing by lawyers and arbitrators depends on practitioners having a clear idea of where the line is drawn between good and bad arbitration practices and that practical guidance on good faith for the legal representatives of the parties is necessary.[16]

In addition to concerns about the so-called uneven playing field and the continued need for the international arbitration system to police itself, there are several other dimensions that ought to be taken into account. One such dimension concerns the involvement of states as parties in both investment and commercial cases, which has added a public interest factor to the equation, particularly as a result of increasing publication of investment awards.

A further consideration is the fact that, although some procedures in international arbitration have evolved into what has been termed "hybridization neutrality", ethical norms are not easy to hybridize.[17] The result has been the sub-surface collision of the ethical rules, sometimes obscured even to the participants in the proceeding.[18] The combination of enhanced transparency and greater public scrutiny of the arbitral procedure with non-transparency in ethics obligations, including the existence of conflicting rules, has created an unstable foundation that may put international arbitration at risk of falling short of the demands of the 21st century.[19]

These concerns are not merely speculative, as was brought to light in three recent rulings of ICSID panels that dealt with applications for recusal of counsel. The decisions have been discussed in some detail elsewhere. Suffice it to recall here that the panels took different approaches to the question of their powers to rule on such applications, and one of the panels made clear that, as an international tribunal, it had no deontological responsibilities over the lawyers. In commenting on the ethical rules under which the lawyer in question acted, as well as the Code of Conduct for Lawyers issued by the Council of the Bars and Laws Societies of the European Union, the panel stated:

> *"This material is valuable to the extent that it reveals common general principles which may guide the Committee. But none of it directly binds the Committee, as an international tribunal. Accordingly, the Committee's consideration of the matter is not, and should not be, based upon a nice reading of any particular code of professional ethics, applicable in any particular national jurisdiction. Such codes may vary in their detailed application. Rather, the Committee must consider what general principles are plainly indispensable for the fair conduct of the proceedings."[20]*

Another panel similarly refuted any deontological responsibilities, stating that:

> *"For an international system … it seems unacceptable for the solution to reside in the individual national bodies which regulate the work of professional service providers, because that might lead to inconsistent or indeed arbitrary outcomes depending on the attitudes of such bodies, or the content (or lack of relevant content) of their rules. It would moreover be disruptive to interrupt international cases to ascertain the position taken by such bodies."*[21]

Against this background, the opportunity to examine the issue of document exchanges and the collision of ethical duties of counsel from different legal systems is welcome.

3. ISSUES RELATED TO WHAT CONSTITUTES ETHICAL COUNSEL CONDUCT IN CONNECTION WITH DOCUMENT EXCHANGES

As is frequently pointed out, the extent of document production by one party to the other party is one of the principal areas of difference between common law and civil law dispute-settlement systems. The differences are particularly pronounced in court proceedings. As may be recalled, in common law systems, parties to court proceedings are required to collaborate in pre-trial discovery of documents. This generally leads to each party having to disclose to the other party all documents in its possession that are relevant to the dispute, except documents that are privileged from production, for instance because of a confidential attorney-client relationship. The obligation to disclose is extensive and covers both documents supportive of the disclosing party's claim and those that are not supportive, including even documents that are adverse to the party presenting them. The broad-ranging discovery process is generally regarded as the only basis on which the truth can be established in cases in which one side has more ready access to the facts underlying the dispute. While this approach has its advantages, a broad discovery process is often criticized for being time consuming and overly expensive.[22]

In civil law systems, parties for the most part produce only those documents on which they intend to rely to prove their case. Although certain documents may be required to be produced, the grounds for such production are narrowly defined, avoiding the characterization sometimes levelled at US-style discovery as "fishing expeditions".[23]

As is generally recognized, international arbitration has been tending towards harmonization, incorporating different elements of both civil and common law systems. In so doing, international arbitration has never embraced the full discovery process allowed in common law systems. Rather, when there is no party agreement on the scope of document disclosure between the parties, the tribunal will generally decide on the extent of disclosure to which the parties will be obligated.[24] It is accepted practice that failure by a party to comply with a production order exposes the party to the risk of the tribunal drawing adverse inferences.[25]

Ethical considerations in international arbitration have in many instances focused on arbitrators. However, as noted above, there is increasing concern about the ethical standards that apply to counsel conduct. In the context of document production, such issues might raise the question of the lawyer's professional obligation in terms of ensuring that documents required to be disclosed are searched for with diligence and, insofar as they are found, disclosed. Another issue is whether counsel have a duty of candour towards the tribunal, requiring full and objective presentation of adverse legal authority. A further question is whether counsel have an obligation of confidentiality when a client's wrongdoing or potential wrongdoing is involved. A different aspect of the question of confidentiality concerns communications generally between attorneys and clients, and the extent to which such communications are protected. As framed by one commentator, "the term 'confidentiality' does not come with a readily definable content".[26] In a discussion of the risk of the so-called "uneven playing field" that may apply to counsel bound by different national ethics standards, one commentator concluded that "there are no readily accessible data from which to draw conclusions about the frequency with which the application of different ethical standards in international arbitration proceedings may result in uneven playing fields".[27] "Indeed," the commentator continued, "there is no data at all on the basis of which one might determine what ethical standards have been applied by any single counsel to any single arbitration."[28] While this is generally true, a review of several investment tribunal decisions provides some, albeit scant, insight into proceedings in which issues implicating counsel conduct have been at play.

4. CASE LAW

a. Search for documents

The question whether a search for documents had been carried out diligently arose in the *Tidewater v. Venezuela* case. In this case, the respondent had stated that it "did not possess, maintain or control" any of the documents sought by the claimants. The respondent observed that, in the context of other cases, "the Republic had made every effort to find relevant documentation from other sources, but said that, unfortunately, those efforts had been unsuccessful".[29] The respondent undertook to conduct a new investigation to confirm that there was nothing to produce and said that it would inform the claimants and the tribunal in due course if the investigation was fruitful. In its ruling, the tribunal decided that the respondent should state which sources "it had so far checked" and undertake a fresh search. The tribunal further decided that:

> *"If documents within the scope of the Claimant's request are discovered in the course of the Respondent's further investigation, the Respondent must produce copies of those documents; save for any which it claims it should be excluded from production on any of the grounds specified under IBA Rule 9. If documents are found which fall within the request, but which the Respondent wishes to exclude from production, it must produce a schedule itemising the documents which it objects to producing, identifying their*

author, date, type of document and the grounds for its objection. In that event, the Claimant may, if it wishes to do so, contest the objection."[30]

The above procedural order suggests that counsel had no duty towards the tribunal independent of the party to the dispute with respect to the outcome of the search for documents. Such a duty is also not stipulated in the Venezuelan Code of Civil Procedure, which in article 436 provides that:

> *"A party seeking to utilize a document that, according to its declaration, lies within the control of the other party, may request its presentation.*
>
> *The request for presentation shall be accompanied by a copy of the document or, failing that, by a statement of the facts known to the requesting party concerning the content of the document and evidence showing that there is at least a serious presumption that the document is or has been within the control of the other party.*
>
> *The court shall require the other party to present or hand over the document within the period it indicates or be subject to a penalty.*
>
> *If the document is not presented within the time-limit fixed and no evidence is provided to show that it does not lie within the control of the other party, the text of the document as it appears in the copy presented by the requesting party shall be presumed to be accurate, or in its absence, the data provided by the requesting party concerning the content of the document shall be deemed to be correct. ..."*[31]

In contrast, US counsel, which appeared for both the claimant and the respondent, might have been influenced by rules which provide as follows.

Rule 3.4(d) of the American Bar Association's Model Rules of Professional Conduct states that:

> "A lawyer shall not: ...
>
> (a) *in* pretrial procedure, *make a frivolous discovery request* or fail to make reasonably diligent effort to comply with a legally proper discovery request by an opposing party;" (emphasis added)

Rule 26(g) of the Federal Rules of Civil Procedure states that:

> "(1) *Every disclosure made pursuant to subdivision (a)(1) or subdivision (a)(3) shall be signed by at least one attorney of record in the attorney's individual name, whose address shall be stated.* An unrepresented party shall sign the disclosure and state the party's address. The signature of the attorney or party constitutes a certification that to the best of the signer's knowledge, information and belief, formed after a reasonable inquiry, the disclosure is complete and correct as of the time it is made.
>
> ...

(3) *If without substantial justification a certification is made in violation of the rule, the court, upon motion or upon its own initiative, shall impose upon the person who made the certification … an appropriate sanction, which may include an order to pay the amount of the reasonable expenses incurred because of the violation, including a reasonable attorney's fee.*" (emphasis added)

It goes beyond the scope or ability of this paper to examine how those differing standards might have been argued or influenced decisions in the *Tidewater* case. Suffice it to say that the duties of counsel under the two national legal systems varied significantly and that, as pointed out above in the *ICC Bulletin*, each side's legal training and experience might have played a role in the manner in which counsel approached the document request.

b. Duty of candour to the arbitral tribunal

One of the questions posed above addressed the issue whether the duty of candour owed to the arbitral tribunal requires a lawyer to bring adverse, controlling authority to the attention of the arbitral tribunal. In the *Generation Ukraine, Inc. v. Ukraine* case, the claimant was taken to task by the tribunal for the way its case had been argued:

> "*[T]he Claimant's written presentation of its case has also been convoluted, repetitive, and legally incoherent. It has obliged the Respondent and the Tribunal to examine a myriad of factual issues which have ultimately been revealed as irrelevant to any conceivable legal theory of jurisdiction, liability or recovery. Its characterization of evidence has been unacceptably slanted, and has required the Respondent and the Tribunal to verify every allegation with suspicion. … The Claimant's position has also been notably inconsistent. … Moreover, the Claimant's presentation of its damages claim has reposed on the flimsiest foundation. … The Claimant's presentation has lacked the intellectual rigour and discipline one would expect of a party seeking to establish a cause of action before an international tribunal.* … Even at the stage of final oral submissions in March 2003, counsel for the Claimant relied on two ICSID awards without mentioning that they had been partially annulled. The Tribunal assumes in counsel's favour that he was unaware of the annulments; that is bad enough, and does no credit to the Claimant."[32] (emphasis added)

While the main criticism of the tribunal was directed at the claimant, counsel conduct was also implicated with respect to certain omissions, implicitly raising the question whether counsel, in the tribunal's view, was bound to bring adverse legal authority to the tribunal's attention or whether counsel was simply required to be more thorough in ascertaining the correctness of legal argument so as to avoid misleading the tribunal.[33] While this particular example is drawn from counsel conduct at the oral hearing, the issue also extends to the written phase of the proceedings and could have a bearing on document exchanges.

c. Confidentiality

The third question posed above concerns the issue whether counsel has an obligation of confidentiality when client wrongdoing or potential wrongdoing is involved. In the *Methanex v. Unites states* case, the tribunal established during the oral hearing that certain documents presented by the claimant "had been obtained by successive and multiple acts of trespass committed by Methanex over five and a half months in order to obtain an unfair advantage over the USA as a Disputing Party to these pending arbitration proceedings".[34] The tribunal took particular offense at the fact that Methanex had applied for the production of certain documents the originals of which it had already collected by unlawful means. The tribunal said that:

> *"[i]t would be wrong to allow Methanex to introduce this documentation into these proceedings in violation of its general duty of good faith and, moreover, that Methanex's conduct, committed during these arbitration proceedings, offended basic principles of justice and fairness required of all parties in every international arbitration."*[35]

Although the tribunal did not reprimand counsel per se, the tribunal noted that the claimant's violation of a general duty of good faith, as imposed by the UNCITRAL Rules, was "incumbent on all who participate in international arbitration, without which it cannot operate", thus articulating a requirement that presumably extended to counsel and raising the question whether good faith requirements in certain circumstances might override obligations of confidentiality.

A related issue arose in the *Cementownia v. Turkey* case, in which the tribunal was called on to deal with the claimant's allegations that the respondent had illegally intercepted certain information and used such surveillance results in the arbitration. In this case, counsel for the respondent provided the arbitral tribunal with assurances that no such intercepts or surveillance results had been received or used in conjunction with the arbitration. The tribunal accepted counsel's assurances and emphasized "the fundamental importance of such a representation to the proper administration of the arbitration".[36] The tribunal went on to impose on both the respondent and its counsel a "continuing duty to ensure that there shall be no use whatsoever of intercepted communications in this arbitration".[37] In this case, the tribunal clearly established a formal role for counsel to ensure accountability for steps taken by the client.

5. CONCLUSION

The above-mentioned cases from the investment arbitration arena show that tribunals have been reluctant to hold counsel appearing in investment arbitrations to particular standards, let alone impose sanctions when the legal representation has fallen short of the tribunal's expectations. Most rulings have been directed to the parties and leave unaddressed the question what role counsel might have played in bringing about a particular situation or shortcoming.

This approach may be partly due to the fact that tribunals do not want to assume deontological responsibilities. Instead, they have relied on arbitral practice under international law to deal with allegations of misconduct of the parties, including failure to arbitrate in good faith. In so doing, tribunals have avoided the issue of the application to counsel of possibly conflicting standards, let alone poorly defined rules of international arbitration. Yet, it is evident that proper counsel conduct is of enormous value to the continued success of international arbitration and that parties, tribunals and counsel would benefit from a clearer understanding of the rules governing counsel conduct.

Endnotes:

1   See *ICC International Court of Arbitration Bulletin—2006 Special Supplement—Document Production in International Arbitration* (November 2006) (hereinafter, *ICC Bulletin*).

2   See P. Tercier, 'Foreword', in *ICC Bulletin*, supra note 1, at p. 5.

3   See B. Hanotiau, 'Document Production in International Arbitration: A Tentative Definition of 'Best Practices', in *ICC Bulletin*, supra note 1, at p. 113.

4   See L. Kimmelman and D. MacGrath, 'Document Production in the United States', in *ICC Bulletin, supra note* 1, at pp. 53-54.

5   See Y. Derains, 'Towards Greater Efficiency in Document Production Before Arbitral Tribunals—A Continental Viewpoint', in *ICC Bulletin, supra* note 1, at p. 83, quoting G. Aguilar-Alvarez, 'To What Extent Do Arbitrators in International Arbitration Disregard the *Bag and Baggage* of National Systems?', *ICCA Congress Series* no. 8 (1998) at p. 139.

6   See A. El-Kosheri and M. Abdel Wahab, 'Trends in Document Production in Egypt and the Arab World', in *ICC Bulletin, supra* note 1, at p. 13.

7   See H. Grigera Naón, 'Document Production in International Commercial Arbitration: A Latin American Perspective', in *ICC Bulletin, supra* note 1, at p. 19.

8   See M. Hwang and A. Chin, 'Discovery in Court and Document Production in International Commercial Arbitration—Singapore', in *ICC Bulletin, supra* note 1, at p. 41.

9   Id.

10   See V.V. Veeder, 'Document Production in England: Legislative Developments and Current Arbitral Practice', in *ICC Bulletin, supra* note 1, at p. 59.

11   Id.

12   Id.

13   See C. Rogers, 'Fit and Function in Legal Ethics: Developing a Code of Conduct for International Arbitration', *Mich. J. Int'l L.* 23 (2002) 341; C. Brower and S. Schill, 'Regulating Counsel Conduct Before International Arbitral Tribunals', in P. Bekker, R. Dolzer and M. Waibel (eds.), *Making Transnational Law Work in the Global Economy: Essays in Honour of Detlev Vagts* (Cambridge University Press 2010); D. Bishop and M. Stevens, 'The Compelling Need for a Code of Ethics in International Arbitration: Transparency, Integrity and Legitimacy', in *ICCA Congress Series* no. 15 (2011).

14   See D. Bishop and M. Stevens, 'International Code of Ethics for Lawyers Practicing Before International Arbitral Tribunals', *ICCA Congress Series* no. 15 (2011); see also P. Sands, 'The ILA Hague Principles on Ethical Standards for Counsel Appearing Before International Courts and Tribunals (Principles developed and issued on authority of co-chairs and working group)', *The Law and Practice of International Courts and Tribunals* 10(1) (2011) at pp. 6-10.

15   See C. Benson, 'Can Professional Ethics Wait? The Need for Transparency in International Arbitration', *Disp. Res. Int'l* 3(1) (2009) at pp. 78-94.

16   See V.V. Veeder, 'The 2001 Goff Lecture—The Lawyer's Duty to Arbitrate in Good Faith', *Arbitration International* 18(4) (2002) at pp. 341-451.

17   See C. Rogers, 'Between Cultural Boundaries and Legal Traditions: Ethics in International Commercial Arbitration', *Bocconi Legal Studies Research Paper* no. 06-1 (2006) at p. 46, available at: <http://ssrn.com/abstract=280850> or <http://dx.doi.org/10.2139/ssrn.280850>.

18   Id., at p. 48.

19   See Bishop and Stevens, *supra* note 13.

20   Unpublished ICSID decision dated 18 September 2008.

21 *Hrvatska Elektroprivreda d.d. v. Republic of Slovenia*, ICSID case no. ARB/05/24, Tribunal's Ruling regarding the participation of David Mildon QC in further stages of the proceedings, 6 May 2008, at para. 23.

22 See L. Reed and J. Sutcliffe, 'The Americanization of International Arbitration?', in *Mealey's International Arbitration Report* 16(4) (2001) at p. 39.

23 Id.

24 See S. Elsing, 'Procedural Efficiency in International Arbitration: Choosing the Best of Both Legal Worlds', *Zeitschrift für Schiedsverfahren (SchiedsVZ)* 3 (2011) at p. 122.

25 Id.

26 See Rogers, *supra* note 13, at p. 371.

27 See Benson, *supra* note 15, at p. 81.

28 Id.

29 *Tidewater, Inc and Others v. Venezuela*, ICSID case no. ARB/10/5, Procedural Order No. 1 on Production of Documents, 29 March 2011, at para. 17.

30 Id., at para. 21.

31 Article 436 of the Venezuelan Code of Civil Procedure, available at <http://www.wtocenter. org.tw/SmartKMS/fileviewer?id=34900>.

32 *Generation Ukraine, Inc. v. Ukraine,* ICSID case no. ARB/00/9, Award, at paras. 24.2-24.7.

33 In this proceeding, counsel representing the claimant was Irish. Article 5.3 of the Code of Conduct for the Bar of Ireland provides as follows: "Barristers must not deceive or knowingly mislead the court. A barrister must take appropriate steps to correct any misleading statement made by the barrister to the court as soon as possible after the barrister becomes aware that the statement was misleading."

34 *Methanex Corporation v. United States*, UNCITRAL, Final Award on Jurisdiction and Merits, Part II, Chapter I: the USA's Application for the Exclusion of Certain of Methanex's Evidence, 3 August 2005, at para. 56.

35 Id., at para. 59.

36 *Cementownia "Nowa Huta" SA v. Turkey,* ICSID case no. ARB(AF)/06/2, Award, 11 September 2009, at para. 44.

37 Id.

CHAPTER THREE

THE ROLE OF USERS

V.V. Veeder

1. INTRODUCTION

The user of arbitration is an important economic, legal and necessary fact. Economically, because it is not the ICC Court of Arbitration that pays the fees and expenses of the arbitrators but the users of international arbitration, and it is also the users who pay the administrative fees of the ICC. And who pays the lawyers as the parties' legal representatives in the arbitration? It is again the users or, increasingly, the users' insurers and funding agents. Legally, because without users as disputing parties there could be no dispute referable to arbitration. Finally, if users settled their disputes amicably, there could be no arbitration or award. In short, users are a necessary fact to every international arbitration: it is their arbitration.

Accordingly, in practice and theory, users and lawyers should share substantially the same interests, because the latter's clients lie at the heart of the arbitration. To a material extent, at least objectively, many of these identical interests are shared by arbitrators and arbitral institutions. In reality, as we all know, this is not quite so.

Increasingly, most one-off users agree to international arbitration unwittingly or with less than fully informed consent. With the emergence of a dispute, users may appear fleetingly at the origin of the arbitration, and they may then attend the first procedural meeting, if held in person, to sign the terms of reference and influence, marginally, the timetable for the arbitration. Thereafter, users generally disappear behind their lawyers into an arbitral form of Siberian exile. It is not that users, in the field of international arbitration, are treated as customers who are always wrong or less than right. It is more a case of the vanishing user, leading to an assumption that users' interests are exactly the same as lawyers' interests. It need not be so—and it used not to be so.

2. THE SEWAGE FARM CASE

My first arbitration, about a sewage farm in the desert many decades ago, took place in a country in the Persian (or Arabian) Gulf. It was a building dispute between the contractor, a well-known local construction company, and the employer, the Ministry of Public Works of that country. There were no factual witnesses, because the two individuals most familiar with and mainly responsible for both the building project and the dispute had been appointed as the two arbitrators for the contractor and the employer, namely the contractor's chief executive officer and the Ministry's chief engineer. The hearing was commendably short, and the arbitration quickly concluded with an award, which unsurprisingly was not unanimous. It seemed to reflect the decision of the third arbitrator, an electrical engineer, who no doubt thought it useful to hear privately, first-hand, from those most knowledgeable about the project and the parties' dispute. The award was fair; and the arbitration was regarded as a success by both users. Because this was my first arbitration, I assumed that this was how most international arbitrations could be conducted: by the users, for the users and, of course, with the informed consent of the users. I soon learnt that this was a very unusual form of arbitration, viewed with horror by most other lawyers who knew of it. Such an arbitration, even by consent of the users, could probably not be held even under existing arbitration rules. Even if it could survive the application of the new ICC Rules, it could not survive the English Arbitration Act 1996, nor French law.[1] And so, over the years, I learnt that international arbitration has surprisingly little to do with users, beginning with the drafting of arbitration agreements long before any dispute. Again, that was not always so.

3. THE BRUNEL CASE

There is an early 19th century case in the English courts about the great Anglo-French architect and engineer, Isambard Kingdom Brunel (1806-1889), the celebrated builder of steamships, bridges, tunnels and railways. He was also a great entrepreneur and businessman, and as the employer (of which he was at least a shareholder), he regularly drafted an early form (almost) of the FIDIC Conditions of Contract. For his grand projects, the agreement between the employer and the contractor appointed in advance as arbitrator of all disputes the engineer nominated by the employer who best knew the employer's mind, namely Brunel. The law reports record a challenge by the contractor against the employer engineer on the basis that the engineer (Brunel) was necessarily dependent upon and partial towards the interests of the employer. That challenge was rejected by the House of Lords, notably because the contractor had agreed to the engineer in advance in the contractual documentation. Given that agreement between the two users and Brunel's undoubted reputation as a true gentleman and a great engineer, the English court was content to leave him to decide all disputes under the agreement.[2] At the time, the idea of appointing the two users as co-arbitrators, let alone one user as sole arbitrator, worked successfully with the users' consent. We probably cannot re-introduce today the practices of those good old days. Form has overtaken substance in many parts of our lives, and arbitration is much more adversarial and is now played for much higher stakes. In a more recent case, we see a different situation where interference in the separate relationships between the users, the lawyers and the arbitrators can prove fatal to an arbitration.

4. THE TURNER CASE

In the *Turner* case, there was a dispute—well known at the time but since happily resolved—about the right of foreign lawyers to represent a foreign party in a Singapore arbitration, without the risk of arrest, injunction or deportation by the Singapore authorities.[3] In that case, the sole arbitrator was also removed for misconduct by the Singapore court. He was an experienced arbitrator (not a lawyer) and a former president of the Chartered Institute of Arbitrators. There were several grounds for a disgruntled party to challenge him, one of which was his attempt to go over the heads of the apparently bickering lawyers and their seemingly interminable procedural wrangles by writing directly to their clients, the users. For that conduct, treated as misconduct but readily understandable in other contexts, this sole arbitrator was admonished and removed from office by the Singapore Court. It seems that the interests of the users in that arbitration were not universally shared by all their lawyers, and that the interests of certain of these lawyers were treated with greater deference by the Singapore Court. It remains a puzzling decision and a cautionary tale: it suggests that an arbitrator should not second-guess the interests of users as represented by their lawyers during the arbitration.

5. ARBITRATION AGREEMENTS

As far as drafting agreements is concerned, we know from practical experience that at the conclusion of successful commercial negotiations, users often pay little attention to the drafting of a specially tailored provision for the best resolution of any future dispute relating to their transaction. Understandably, the parties appear to take legal advice late, and then those lawyers choose a standard system of dispute resolution, readily available and easily known to them as arbitration rules, the ICC, LCIA, IRDC, SCC, SIAC or, increasingly, UNCITRAL. This significantly reduces the risk of pathological arbitration clauses; but it has also removed the influence of users on the drafting of their own arbitration clauses in favour of standard form arbitration rules that have traditionally been drafted by lawyers, not users.

In recent times there have been several attempts to involve users, most notably by those responsible for drafting the new ICC Rules.[4] What is surprising is that when users are consulted on the drafting of arbitration rules, they seem to be conservative and cautious. In recent rule reforms, users have significantly not insisted upon or even proposed radical changes to arbitration rules. For example, let us look at the factors that affect users most in any arbitration: the heavy costs, efforts, disruption and delays of wide-ranging document production (or "discovery"). Why do none of the most used arbitration rules provide for arbitration without any form of document production? Why is it that before a dispute users still seem more concerned to have in existence a rule-based right to document production rather than specially tailored procedural rules more appropriate to their particular transaction, trade or future dispute? We know that this point was raised in the reform of the new ICC Rules, but users, when consulted, preferred the safety of familiar habits. Or is this, again, a case of users consulting their own lawyers and identifying their views and interests with theirs out of an abundance of caution?

6. ORAL HEARINGS

Under many domestic arbitration rules, small claims procedures preclude oral hearings and/or oral witnesses and require the dispute to be decided on written submissions only, by consent of the users expressed in advance of their dispute. In London, the LMAA Small Claims Procedure has proved successful with both domestic and international users of maritime arbitration in London. This is obviously not a procedure for large claims—nor indeed for complex small claims—but why is it assumed by users to be inapplicable to all other international disputes? Given the high costs of hearings in international arbitrations, why is it so rare to see an arbitration conducted without hearings or at least without any oral witnesses? Hearings add massively to the costs of an arbitration, and it is a sad fact of life that many lawyers will advise a client not to pursue a claim by means of international arbitration if the amount is less than a certain figure. In London, 10 years ago, we inquired of several City firms what this figure was for ICC and LCIA arbitrations. It ranged between USD 3 and USD 5 million then; and it must be higher now. If so, this is regrettable. It does not seem right for claimants to be disenfranchised from making relatively small claims by means of international arbitration, and it seems more than regrettable that a possible cure, an adjusted procedure, could not be developed to make international arbitration possible even for very small claims. Something seems to be wrong. If the most ambitious solutions cannot prevail, let us start with a relatively small reform.

7. CAPPED COSTS

For many users, the new imperative is to win their arbitration at almost any cost. The allocation of costs against the losing party by the tribunal is therefore an important weapon in the arbitral armoury that few users would wish to abandon (the so-called ABBA principle: "the winner takes it all"). However, as regards costs incurred from the first procedural meeting to the award, we again see the absence of users' direct input in the arbitration process. This is even more surprising given that every international arbitration conducted between users and lawyers of different background is itself an exercise in comparative procedure, requiring flexibility, compromise and a methodology best suited to that particular arbitration. There should therefore be an important role for all users as regards costs: not only the costs of the arbitrators and the arbitral institution but also the far greater legal costs and expenses payable to the users' own lawyers, experts and witnesses, all compounded twice over by the application of the loser-pays-costs rule.

Why not, therefore, place a user-agreed cap on the total legal costs of the arbitration at the outset of the arbitration? This cap could work in two ways. For large claims, it would at least prepare both sides at the outset (i.e., the actual users as distinct from their lawyers) for what could be a significantly high bill for legal costs (compounded twice over). The mutual of that potential liability could persuade parties to come to an amicable settlement. In more modest cases, where the quantum of the claim is relatively low, it would be important for the users to decide at the outset, by agreement with the tribunal, to keep legal costs at a level proportionate to the amount of the claim. It is notorious that, for a relatively modest claim raising no fundamental principles, users can spend a far greater sum in legal costs to recover the lesser sum in dispute.

Such cost-capping was introduced in England under sections 63 and 65 of the Arbitration Act 1996. Under section 63, parties are free to agree what costs of the arbitration are recoverable as between themselves; and under section 65, unless otherwise agreed by the parties, the tribunal may direct that the recoverable costs of the arbitration (or any part of such costs) shall be limited to a specified amount.[5] The first provision depends upon the parties' consent, but the second depends on the tribunal only, with no need for the parties' consent. There was no counterpart to these provisions in the 1985 UNCITRAL Model Law, and the Department advisory Committee (DAC) on the Law of Arbitration recorded its legislative intentions, as follows:

"We consider that such a power, properly used, could prove to be extremely valuable as an aid to reducing unnecessary expenditure. It also represents a facet of the duty of the tribunal as set out in Clause 33 [i.e., the tribunal's mandatory duty 'to adopt procedures suitable to the circumstances of the particular case avoiding unnecessary delay or expense...']. This power enables the tribunal to put a ceiling on costs, so that while a party can continue to spend as much as it likes on an arbitration it will not be able to recover more than the ceiling limit from the other party. This will have the added virtue of discouraging those who wish to use their financial muscle to intimidate their opponents into giving up through fear that by going on they might be subject to a costs order which they could not sustain."[6]

This provision in section 65 has been used surprisingly little by English tribunals. The same applies to the use of section 63 by parties, but in recent difficult economic times there was renewed interest in its application.[7]

In 2009, the London Maritime Arbitrators' Association (LMAA) in its new Intermediate Claims Procedure (ICP) for LMAA arbitration disputes addressing claims between USD 50,000 and USD 400,000. This procedure provides for a specific cap on legal costs: "The parties' recoverable costs are to be capped so that neither party shall be entitled to recover more than the sum equivalent to 30% of the claimant's monetary claims as advanced plus the amount of a counterclaim, if any." If there is an oral hearing, the percentage increases from 30% to 50%. This new provision concludes: "These percentages are maximum figures, and the tribunal may at any time in its absolute discretion cap the parties' future costs so that the total cap amounts to some lesser percentage than is here stated." Could similar cost-capping work for international arbitrations? It could certainly provide an element of confidence for users who are nervous about the allocation of legal costs according to the loser-pays principle or about the disproportionate amount of legal costs. For ICC arbitrations, the initiative would have to start by consent with tribunals and parties at the first procedural meeting in clearly appropriate cases. However, if it did work in practice, it could be considered in the future as a possible change to the new ICC Rules and other arbitration rules currently being revised by other institutions.

8. CONCLUSION

But could this really work in practice? Can any major reform ever be introduced by users of international arbitration? The likely fate of the LMAA's ICP rules may provide a salutary lesson: they are about to be abolished as a result of opposition by maritime users. This is the place where, it seems, the interests of users and lawyers do diverge, not for reasons of self-interest or financial greed, but because users are essentially even more cautious and even more uncomfortable than lawyers with what is unknown, unfamiliar and as yet unproven—all traits that bend towards orthodoxy rather than radicalism. As St Augustine, here the patron saint of arbitral users (almost) said: "Grant me innovation and reform in the new ICC Rules, only not yet."

Endnotes:

1 See, for example, the recent decision of the Cour d'appel de Reims of 2 November 2011 in *Avax v. Tecnimont*.

2 *Ranger v. Great Western Railway Co.* (1854) 5 HL Cas 72, 10 ER 824 (HL).

3 *In the Matter of an Arbitration between Builders Federal (Hong Kong) Limited and. Joseph Gartner & Co. v. Turner (East Asia) Pte Ltd* (1988); see also Michael Polkinghorne, 'The Right of Representation in a Foreign Venue' *Arbitration International* 4 (1988) p. 333.

4 The high-water mark among modern arbitration rules was contained in the LCIA's 1985 Rules: "The parties may agree on the conduct of their arbitral proceedings and they are encouraged to do so…" (now Article 14.1 of the LCIA's 1998 Rules).

5 Section 65 states simply: "Unless otherwise agreed by the parties, the tribunal may direct that the recoverable costs of the arbitration, or any part of the arbitral proceedings, shall be limited to a specified amount. Any direction may be made or varied at any stage, but it must be done sufficiently in advance of the incurring of costs to which it relates, or the taking of any steps in the proceedings which may be affected by it, for the limit to be taken into account."

6 See the DAC's First Report (January 1996) para. 272; Mustill & Boyd: Commercial Arbitration: 2001 Companion Volume (2001) p. 439.

7 It has attracted attention even outside England. See Daniel Wehrli, 'Zum Höhe und Umfang erstattungsfähiger Parteikosten', *DIS-Materialen X* (2005) pp. 77-78.

CHAPTER FOUR

IN-HOUSE COUNSEL: WHY THEY SHOULD BE MORE INVOLVED IN THE ARBITRAL PROCESS

Karl Hennessee

There is an expression in German—*Glück im Unglück*—that means "fortune in misfortune". Just the other day, I was fortunate to have a bit of misfortune that aptly illustrates why the value that the participation of a user can add to an arbitration is maximized by consistent, constructive involvement.

I would like to share an anecdote. I am currently involved in an English-language arbitration in Germany that is neither large nor complicated. In fact, it seemed to be running along smoothly until the only phenomenon that is perhaps more dangerous than the "vanishing client", as mentioned in V.V. Veeder's contribution to this dossier, occurred, namely the appearance of the "submarine client". The "submarine client" is a client that unpredictably appears and disappears from any given matter. In this particular example, the submarine client made his first appearance only after the terms of reference and the procedural order had been agreed, in which it had been decided that document production was unnecessary in a case that was fundamentally about an interpretation of German law. Adding to the attractiveness of this anecdote for present purposes, the submarine client made his appearance in the guise of another perennial favourite of conferences like this: the American lawyer. The submarine's client's first (and so far only) contribution to this matter was to object to the position of his own German lawyer.

The submarine client once again sank beneath the surface, leaving his poor German counsel to try to explain why, despite his prior agreement, he suddenly considered imperative extensive document production, cross-examination and lots of other things that people, sometimes unfairly, tend to believe are the preference of American lawyers. In this case, it remains to be seen whether these procedural adornments will actually prove useful to the tribunal in resolving the dispute at hand. What is clear, however, is that client involvement in this matter would have avoided the extra time, additional cost and general puzzlement of all concerned. The apparent miscommunication between client and counsel and, as a result, with opposing counsel and the tribunal is not the point. Let this anecdote serve instead as an advertisement for the start-to-finish involvement of users—meaning in-house counsel and their business clients—in arbitration.

In my own practice, I always either attend or encourage people in my team to attend procedural hearings, because I believe that the client's involvement is absolutely necessary even, and especially, in the procedural aspects of our practice. In a recent speech, Professor Albert van den Berg even suggested that the client's participation in procedural hearings be mandatory. I would hope that it will not be necessary to order participation in a process when the advantages of user involvement in terms of substantive dispute resolution and procedural cost savings along the way are so clear. In any case, I welcome Professor van den Berg's encouragement of attendance at procedural hearings as a way of getting the client involved. Perhaps it will help to prevent the kind of "fortunate and unfortunate" experience that I recently encountered.

The theme of this paper is mythology. Mythology is convenient, even when we know it is not true, because sometimes we wish that it were true. We continue to rely upon mythology as a convenient way of explaining why the dysfunction of the process is not really "our fault". As a user, speaking on behalf of users, I wish to take partial responsibility for that dysfunction and declare that users are not alone.

In a recent study carried out at Queen Mary, there were two salient statistics that jumped out at me. The first was that there is an 81% preference in a forced-rank analysis for a "fair and just result". That is true. Clients are not just looking to win. They are looking for a fair and just result that allows them to continue their business. This is the well-known statistic, because everyone likes to cite it.

The other statistic relates to the fact that clients are quite willing to take responsibility for causing problems in international arbitration. In the same study, approximately 60% of users take responsibility for problems. Digging deeper into the study, we also find that, while 60% of users willingly (if anonymously) admit to being at the origin of "problems", they still look to arbitral institutions to solve those problems for them. Despite being less well known, this statistic should not be considered surprising either.

A familiar theoretical explanation for this phenomenon comes from the science of economics, where it is described as collectively irrational outcomes based on individual rational decisions. This is frequently borne out in practice. It is entirely rational for a party that benefits from the status quo to delay the proceedings and make them more expensive. Why? Because, with exceptions and all other things being equal, the cost of the pending arbitration to the claimant in pure business terms encourages a settlement more favourable to a respondent who benefits from a favourable status quo.

Let us give business users the benefit of the doubt and assume that they are always as right as they think they are and, therefore, that it is their opponents who must be wrong. Thus, it is the business users who are generally the victims (and certainly never the perpetrators!) of tactics aimed at delaying procedures and increasing costs. It is therefore logical that those who are right would look to arbitrators and arbitral institutions to interfere with the plans of those who employ such tactics. The mythology that governs applies here is that the users will be able to settle such problems among themselves. This is no different, for example, than expecting the polluters of the world to get together and actually agree to stop polluting. No, the reason the cap and trade system was invented is because the polluters of the world will always seek to take advantage of a situation that allows them to do pollute. Hence, we are also faced with the tragedy of the international arbitration commons. I regret to share with you the fact that the global community of users understands the weaknesses in the system and arbitrators' tolerance for their exploitation in the name of due process. In their weaker moments, users are perfectly willing to exploit these weaknesses to the extent that arbitrators give them the opportunity to do so.

The first thing that we can do in order to prevent users (who, of course, are always right) and their opponents (who, of course, are always wrong) from actually being allowed to exploit those opportunities is to be involved. Encouraging involvement is the job of other clients as well as of outside counsel and arbitrators. A user who is present in the room and sees the destructive potential that is available (at the direction but also on the responsibility of the user) will probably show a tendency to avoid it in most cases.

On the one hand, we regularly note that arbitration enjoys a positive reputation among our clients, which is true. However, that reputation can occasionally be too positive, because it takes the form of unjustified expectations. Again, the solution is more client involvement. In all arbitrations, but especially when I have a wilful business client, I try to actually involve my business client in the process. I have a reasonably good understanding through experience and study of how the arbitral process works, but I find that some of my business clients are more reactive to a live view of the process than to counselling about it from a distance. So, to take a step further just beyond the legal counsel that may or may not be involved in the arbitration, there are the business people who rely on the result of the arbitration and for whom the fair and just result is actually the point.

Getting business people involved in the process can help them better understand the value of a complete and unqualified result, but, far more importantly, it can help them understand how legal processes can have a negative impact on relationships as a result of their failure to be involved. Nearly 100% of the arbitrations in which I have participated concern long-term relationships, and nearly 100% of the long-term relationships in some industries are maybe based not so much on choice as on the fact that players have no choice but to trust and work with each other. Arbitration is the expression of an opportunity to try to fix a dysfunctional relationship. If we choose not to be involved in that process, we should not be surprised when the process does not satisfy our clients.

Privacy and confidentiality are another reason that some of us choose to get involved in arbitration. Of course, there is the obvious interest in preserving the confidentiality of an elective form of dispute resolution. At the same time, privacy and confidentiality have a price, because sometimes what is communicated in the hearing room does not make its way back to the client. What I try to do for those clients who cannot be involved in the hearings themselves is to take back to them the information that I have heard. Predicting the result based on whether arbitrator

X or arbitrator Y nodded knowingly or smiled during a particular line of questioning is not the point. Rather, the focus is to help business clients understand how the dynamic of the process itself will help the settlement of the dispute. I personally find that my clients are most satisfied with the arbitrations in which they have participated. In fact, they often seem more satisfied when they have participated in arbitrations where we were not successful in getting what we claimed than in arbitrations where we were 100% successful but in which they did not actually participate. The difference is the appreciation of the various functions of the process beyond the simple resolution of a disputed point.

Accelerated settlement dynamics are another useful consequence of user participation in arbitration. One phenomenon whose significance is not always appreciated is that, while the outside counsel of the parties usually remain distant from one another, the in-house counsel and the witnesses meeting in hearings feel an immediate need to come together and discuss. That does more to foster settlements in the line of fire than perhaps anything else any actor in the arbitral community can do. Bringing users together and giving them a reason to overcome the irrational fear of appearing "weak" (by being the one to reach out to discuss settlement) is something that the arbitral hearings are quite successful at fostering. In other words, since both sides have to be there, why not take the opportunity to release the arbitrators of the obligation of settling the dispute by agreeing that this is really unnecessary in view of the evidence that has been presented.

Outside counsel and arbitrators have their own mythology. Outside lawyers will tend to believe that they have been hired to replace in-house counsel in arbitral proceedings. That is simply not accurate: they are part of a team, not the whole team. In some cases, in-house counsel may fear that they do not know enough about the process to feel that they can contribute. Their views about the relationships and the long-term business perspective are nonetheless absolutely vital to the successful outcome of the process, whether that outcome is achieved through a settlement or through the dispute being resolved through an award. In any case, from a risk-management perspective, non-engaged clients may present outside counsel with non-responsiveness or an inaccurate presentation of the risk to the business. In such cases, encouraging client participation is especially vital, not least because the client has a less developed understanding of the process.

Those in-house counsel who do have an understanding of the process may have some procedural and substantial ideas to contribute as well. Thus, external counsel should not be afraid or feel abused by clients. The are entitled to a frank discussion with their clients about their expectations regarding their participation at the outset rather than just receiving the factual information they need. This may also make things easier when they have to send their clients a disappointing award and a very large bill.

Arbitrators may also buy into mythology. One such myth is that what users of the system want is an award. In fact, what they are looking for is a result, which comprises the process as well as the award. Yes, a fair and just result does describe the award, but it is also much more than that. I have already described some of the ways in which a well-run process forms a large part of the value that users are "buying". Let me give you one more example. For us, the award serves as a kind of long-term interpretive guide to the contract that formed the subject of a dispute. It is not at all uncommon for a well-written award—one that has carefully considered the issues—to serve as a basis for the resolution of later disputes between the parties for many years. The award takes on the role of a kind of supplementary guide to the contract, which is not something for which court judgments are frequently used. Arbitrators who understand this will serve the interests of the users best by taking the time to weigh the evidence and actually write about their thought processes.

This reality may weigh against the traditional wisdom (or myth) that the speediest award is *always* best. While there is value in an award that comes quickly, there is also value in an award that is thoughtful and perhaps more analytical than one that is simply necessary to resolve the dispute. There is a false economy in always and exclusively pushing arbitrators to render the quickest possible award. It may be necessary under some circumstances but removes the opportunity for a more comprehensive resolution of the issues between the parties. One size does not fit all. Speed is important in certain disputes. Good arbitrators will pick up on the vibe between the parties to determine whether one party is perhaps exploiting the status quo and lengthening the process while another party favours a speedy resolution of the process. The right balance between a timely award and thoughtful reasoning can only be struck on a case-by-case basis. The arbitrators and institutions to whom the users look for help will be the ones who strike the right balance between the value of a speedy award and the value of more thoughtful reasoning. Either, or both, may be the key to saving the relationship between the two parties.

I have shared these thoughts in one form or another—in individual discussions, at conferences and even in publications such as this one—for years. I continue to do so because I believe that participation is very important. I suppose that, in this regard, I am so far meeting Churchill's definition of success, which is to go from failure to failure without the loss of enthusiasm.

CHAPTER FIVE

THE TRIBUNAL'S RIGHTS AND DUTIES: WHAT DO PARTIES AND ARBITRATORS BARGAIN FOR?

Julian D.M. Lew, QC

1. WHOSE ARBITRATION IS IT: PARTIES' OR ARBITRATORS'?

What do parties want from arbitrators? What do arbitrators want from the parties? Are they compatible?

This paper suggests that parties want efficient, independent, reliable and impartial arbitrators to determine their differences. They expect the tribunal to establish the facts, determine the law and apply it, remain unbiased, objective and fair throughout the process, and keep the arbitration confidential. They want a tribunal that can manage and conduct the arbitration effectively, act without undue delay and deliver valid decisions. However, the selection of arbitrators is more complicated. Often parties may want arbitrators who they think may be more flexible, pliant and willing to accept delays or who they believe may be receptive to different arguments and procedures.

Arbitrators' principal duty is to resolve disputes by determining the respective rights and obligations of the parties. In return for completing their mission, parties have an obligation to remunerate the arbitrators. The arbitrators' right to remuneration is widely recognized in international arbitration. Yet, in the decision-making process, tribunals may be called to fulfil tasks that suggest that other entitlements may be derived from the arbitration mandate. Do arbitrators have the right to act without threat, harassment and pressure? Do they enjoy the right not to be called as witnesses in subsequent proceedings? Can they resign when circumstances dictate such course of action? Do arbitrators have any other rights in addition to payment? Do arbitrators have a right to exercise their powers as arbitrators, for example, to call for evidence or for the attendance of witnesses, appoint experts? The main question is: what do arbitrators and parties bargain for in the dispute resolution process?

In addition to being paid, arbitrators also hope and expect that parties and their counsel will provide clear arguments and all relevant supporting evidence and authorities. This will assist them to reach their determinations. Arbitrators invariably hope that the arbitration will be conducted in a professional and courteous manner. Arbitrators would prefer not to be involved with or embroiled in disputes between counsel, be copied on inter-counsel correspondence or find themselves an object of counsel's aggression.

A close look into the relationship between parties and arbitrators shows a shift of power during the arbitral process from the parties to the arbitrators. At the outset of the arbitral process, the parties retain control: they select the tribunal, can agree on the applicable law, decide on the procedure and timetable, and fix the seat and language of the proceedings. After the arbitration is set in motion, the arbitrators' control over the process grows exponentially. Ultimately, the arbitrators take command by deciding procedural issues that may arise and cannot be agreed, ordering production of documents where appropriate, determining the evidence considered relevant, conducting the hearings, establishing the facts, applying the law and delivering the award. Some might say that is real power.

Arbitrators' duties develop in connection with their powers and gravitate around due process, fairness and completing the parties' mandate. The rights of arbitrators derive not only from the contractual nature of arbitration but also from their adjudicatory function. Perhaps more subtle or less visible than their powers, these rights aim at ensuring that the same principles of fairness and due process intended to protect the parties also protect the arbitrators. The key factor is that at the end of the process, absent settlement, the arbitrators determine the issues and their decision is final.

This paper considers three issues: first, how the relationship between the parties and the arbitrators is determined; second, arbitrators' duties towards the parties; and, third, arbitrators' rights.

2. THE RELATIONSHIP BETWEEN THE PARTIES AND THE ARBITRATOR

Arbitrators derive their mandate from the parties' agreement, the arbitration rules, the terms of appointment or the applicable arbitration law. In recognition of the arbitrators' lack of coercive authority, national laws confer on them certain powers of direction and control of the process and facilitate access to court assistance where needed. Paradoxically, national law and institutional rules almost never deal with the status of the arbitrators and the nature of their relationship with the parties.[1] Notwithstanding the legal controls, it is widely recognized that, most of the time, the relationships between the arbitrators and the parties, and their respective rights and obligations, have a contractual nature.[2] In addition, mandatory requirements under national laws operating as prerequisites of any dispute resolution system may have a bearing on arbitrators' duties.[3]

a. Contractual arrangement

I. ARBITRATION AGREEMENT

The arbitration agreement is the primary source for arbitrators' authority. Arbitrators and parties enter into an agreement, directly or indirectly, sometimes called the *arbitrator's contract*, whereby both sides assume reciprocal obligations in exchange for certain rights. The arbitrator's contract can be express—when parties actually sign an agreement with the arbitrator (i.e., terms of appointment)—or implied—by accepting appointment (e.g., under applicable arbitration rules and/or national law).

The nature of the arbitrator's contract has stirred strong conceptual debates. It has been qualified as an agency contract,[4] a contract for services[5] or a sui generis contract "not being categorizable in conventional terms and instead giving rise to a unique set of rights and duties".[6] In the recent *Jivraj v. Hashwani* decision,[7] the UK Supreme Court qualified the arbitrator as an "independent provider of services who is not in a relationship of subordination with the parties who receive his services".[8] The Supreme Court noted that the arbitrator's role is to be independent from both parties. The arbitrator is not subordinated to any party; on the contrary, the nature of his function requires him to "rise above the partisan interests of the parties and not to act in, or so as to further, the particular interests of either party. … He is in effect a 'quasi-judicial adjudicator'…".[9]

II. ARBITRATION RULES

When the arbitration agreement contains a reference to the rules of an arbitral institution, the arbitrator's rights and duties will be defined by those arbitration rules. In institutional arbitration, the relationship between those involved is trilateral. The institution enters into a contract with the parties when it accepts the case. It also enters into a separate (yet related) contractual relationship with the arbitrator via appointment and/or confirmation of appointment. Through this tripartite relationship, the institution's rules become part of the arbitrator's contract and may affect various aspects of the arbitrator's rights (e.g., remuneration), powers (e.g., the power to order security for costs) and duties (e.g., the duty to present the draft award to the institution for scrutiny before releasing it to the parties). There may be subtle and substantive differences between rules of different institutions giving greater or lesser authority, duties and powers to arbitrators. If there is a dispute between parties and arbitrators, it will generally be determined (at least at first instance) by the institution.

III. TERMS OF APPOINTMENT

The terms of appointment define the arbitrator's rights, powers and duties in ad hoc arbitration. They are also common practice in some legal systems, notably in maritime, insurance and other arbitrations in England. The terms of appointment typically confirm the arbitrator's appointment and the financial arrangements (appointment and booking fees, hourly and daily rates, deposits, interim billing, fees in the event of settlement, cancellations and adjournments, and expenses). They may also deal with certain procedural aspects of arbitration: conflicts, the arbitrator's right to appoint assistants, governing law, document retention, and so forth.

Terms of appointment are signed by the parties and the arbitrators and are usually final. Disputes related to the terms of appointment are typically deferred to courts. For example, where arbitrators sought during the arbitration process to impose a cancellation fee formula that had been rejected by one of the parties at the outset of the arbitration, the court considered that they had misused their position and removed the arbitrators.[10]

IV. APPLICABLE ARBITRATION LAW

When the arbitration agreement is silent or does not set down in detail the arbitrators' mandate, the applicable arbitration law defines their rights, powers and duties. For example, if parties agree to arbitration in England, it is reasonable to assume that the arbitration will be governed by the English Arbitration Act 1996. In particular, sections 33 and 34 of the Act complete the arbitrator's mandate. Section 33 provides for the general duty to act fairly and give each party a reasonable opportunity of presenting its arguments and to adopt procedures suitable to the circumstances of each case. Section 34 details the procedural and evidentiary matters to be decided by the arbitrators.

Because of the numerous ways in which an arbitration can be conducted, the applicable arbitration laws can often embrace general formulas. Under the principle of party autonomy, parties can supplement or depart from the provisions of the applicable law. However, their freedom is limited where the relevant provisions are mandatory. In this context, the DAC Report (published with the Arbitration Act 1996) notes:

> "It seems to us that the public interest dictates that Clause 33 must be mandatory i.e. that the parties cannot effectively agree to dispense with the duty laid on arbitrators under Clause 33. In other words, they cannot effectively agree that the arbitrators can act unfairly, or that the arbitrators can be partial, or that the arbitrators can decide that the parties (or one of them) should not have a reasonable opportunity of putting his case or answering that of his opponent, or indeed that the arbitrators can adopt procedures that are unsuitable for the particular circumstances of the case or are unnecessarily slow or expensive, so that the means for resolving the matters to be determined is unfair."[11]

Where parties agree on procedures that in their view conform to the mandatory provisions of the applicable law but the arbitrators do not share the same view, it is, as the DAC drafters noted, "neither desirable nor practicable to stipulate that the tribunal can override the agreement of the parties".[12]

b. Legal requirements—law governing the arbitration

The law governing the arbitration may have an impact on the arbitrators' mandate even when parties explicitly define it in the arbitration agreement. In fulfilling their role, the arbitrators must be mindful of the mandatory legal provisions impacting the conduct of the proceedings and the substantive law. For example, if there is a local time requirement or form of award, or if there is some other requirement as to how the arbitrators should conduct the arbitration, they should be careful to comply with it. This is not easy where arbitrators are from different jurisdictions and may not know or be fully conversant with the content and details of the *lex arbitri*. This imposes an obligation on counsel to bring any such legal requirements to the attention of the tribunal.

3. ARBITRATOR'S DUTIES TOWARDS THE PARTIES

The arbitrator has five main duties to the parties: (1) to determine the dispute between the parties; (2) to stay impartial and independent; (3) to conduct the arbitration fairly and without undue delay; (4) to keep the arbitration confidential; and (5) to deliver an enforceable award. There are of course other duties that come under some of these headings, but this paper will focus only on those five.

a. The duty to determine the dispute between the parties

First and most obviously, the arbitrators' main duty is to determine the dispute between the parties. In doing so, it is generally accepted that, unless otherwise agreed by the parties, arbitrators may conduct the proceedings as they see fit. They may establish the facts, apply the law and "conduct the arbitration in such a way that it leads to a valid award not open to challenges".[13] It is open to question whether, in fulfilling this function, the arbitrator must limit the decision-making process to the parties' submissions or whether he or she has the power to conduct the proceedings as deemed appropriate under the circumstances.

For example, article 22(2) of the ICC Arbitration Rules (2012) provides that "the arbitral tribunal, after consulting the parties, may adopt such procedural measures as it considers appropriate". Article 25 of the ICC Rules mandates the arbitrators to determine the facts "by all appropriate means". This may include reviewing pleadings, briefs, summaries,[14] documentary and oral evidence, ordering document production[15] and calling its own experts.[16] Other arbitration rules explicitly provide for arbitrators' power to take evidence. Article 14.2 of the LCIA Rules of Arbitration provides that:

> *"[u]nless otherwise agreed by the parties ... the Arbitral Tribunal shall have the widest discretion to discharge its duties allowed under such law(s) or rules of law as the Arbitral Tribunal may determine to be applicable; and at all times the parties shall do everything necessary for the fair, efficient and expeditious conduct of the arbitration."*

On the same topic, article 27(4) of the UNCITRAL Rules of Arbitration allows arbitrators to determine the admissibility, relevance, materiality and weight of the evidence offered. Sometimes, in the absence of evidence rules, arbitrators are allowed to evaluate the evidence "freely", for example, in Sweden.[17]

The way the arbitrators conduct the proceedings should not contradict the parties' agreement and must ensure that their equality and the right to be heard are safeguarded at all stages of the arbitral process.[18] Ultimately, as section 33 of the English Arbitration Act provides, the arbitrators should be mindful of "avoiding unnecessary delay or expense so as to provide a fair means for the resolution of the matters falling to be determined". This is not always easy to do where the parties are seeking different procedural and evidentiary rights (e.g., to submit additional submissions and evidence) and issues are complicated.

In essence, the power to set the appropriate procedure has been interpreted as including: (1) taking control over establishing the facts; (2) proof of substantive law; (3) appointment and instruction of experts; (4) assistance with settlement; (5) limiting time for oral argument and witness examination; and (6) issuing awards and bifurcation of determinative issues.[19]

Applying the law is closely linked to arbitrators' adjudicatory function. Arbitrators are called to make final and binding awards, which they should decide either in accordance with the applicable law (except where the parties have expressly agreed that they should decide *ex aequo et bono* or as *amiables compositeurs*) or taking into account the contract terms and trade usages.[20] Under certain legal systems, the arbitrator is deemed to know the law (*iura novit curia*), while in other jurisdictions (particularly in countries following common law traditions) parties have a duty to prove and argue the law.[21] Applying the law has been interpreted to refer not only to the substantive law of the contract or the contract itself but also to any mandatory law provisions having an impact on the case.[22] For some, this also means taking criminal rules into consideration.[23] For others, the arbitrators should take a "pro-active approach, especially if there is more than one law that could be applied".[24] Yet, it is clear that applying the law does not mean complying with agreements, procedures or rules "that are unlawful or that, in the arbitrator's judgment, would be inconsistent with this [AAA/ABA] Code"[25] or would allow for concealing illicit behaviour.

Delivering the award entails addressing all matters raised by the parties, including those that "seem unimportant or peripheral",[26] and determining all connected disputes. In making the award, the arbitrators should carefully assess the limits of their mandate under the arbitration agreement or the applicable rules or law. Exceeding their authority or addressing matters not contemplated by the parties may have unwanted consequences, varying from remanding the award to the tribunal (where the *lex arbitri* so allows), supplying grounds for annulment[27] or refusal of recognition and enforcement.

b. Duty to stay impartial and independent

In 1799, George Washington wrote in his will that "all disputes (if unhappily any should arise) shall be decided by three impartial and intelligent men, known for their probity and good understanding; two to be chosen by the disputants—each having the choice of one—and the third by those two".[28] Over two centuries later, international arbitrators must guide their conduct by similar values and maintain their independence and impartiality during the arbitral process.

Impartiality and independence are qualities established in most arbitration rules, domestic laws, codes of ethics, international conventions and the IBA Guidelines on Conflicts of Interest in International Arbitration. Some instruments refer to only one of the two concepts. Notwithstanding, when arbitration rules make reference to either independence or impartiality, practice seems to have evolved towards implying both. For example, section 33(1)(a) of the English Arbitration Act provides that the arbitrators "shall act fairly and impartially as between the parties". This provision has been interpreted as encompassing both impartiality and independence, due to England's adoption of the European Convention of Human Rights.[29]

Without intending to discuss or review the meaning of these concepts, independence can essentially be defined as the absence of an actual or past dependent relationship likely to affect the arbitrator's freedom of judgment. Independence entails an objective enquiry into the connections, relations or dealings between the arbitrator and the parties. Impartiality is a state of mind. It means that the arbitrator does not favour one party (i.e., is not biased) and that the arbitration is not pre-decided as to the question(s) in dispute. It is a "fairly abstract and subjective standard".[30]

In general, when challenging the independence or impartiality of an arbitrator, "it is … sufficient to show that there is enough 'doubt' or 'suspicion' … to justify either not appointing or removing the arbitrator".[31] The LCIA Court recently confirmed that the notion of independence is applied "as an objective test for the existence of circumstances that create the appearance of potential bias on the part of the arbitrator".[32] When, on the other hand, the challenge questions impartiality, the LCIA Court applies "a test for the actual presence of bias … as demonstrated by the actions of the arbitrator, rather than simply by the appearance of potential bias."[33] Both standards are applied from the angle of a "fair minded and informed observer".[34]

Arbitrators have a duty to disclose those circumstances giving rise to conflicts of interest prior to accepting a nomination or as soon as it becomes known during the proceedings. They must be careful not to do anything that might affect or give the parties reason to be concerned about their impartiality and independence. Disclosures of actual and potential conflicts should be made as early as possible and must include all relevant facts—both public and private information.[35] Current trends in international arbitration suggest that when in doubt the arbitrator should disclose.[36] Failure to comply can result in challenge and removal of the arbitrator and may occasionally go as far as to trigger annulment of the award or a refusal to enforce the award and perhaps even civil liability on the part of the arbitrator.[37]

c. The duty to conduct the arbitration fairly and without undue delay

Arbitrators have a duty to conduct the arbitral process in a fair manner, giving each party an equal opportunity to be heard and respond to the opponent's submissions. Whether this is a full opportunity as required under the UNCITRAL Model Law,[38] a reasonable opportunity under English law,[39] a "pertinent and material to the controversy" opportunity under the Federal Arbitration Act,[40] or an opportunity to ensure, in the language of the New York Convention, that the party is "[able] to present his case",[41] is a pedantic question.

Fairness is a subjective standard[42] and accordingly varies from one case to another. What may seem fair in one dispute may not meet the test in a different set of circumstances. Fairness is reflected at procedural level by granting the parties a sufficient opportunity to present and argue their case, including the presentation of documentary and testamentary evidence. This includes the right to comment on and rebut the other party's evidence, the right to call witnesses and experts and the right to have a hearing if so required by the parties or called for by the circumstances. More controversial is the right to request documents from the other party.

To expedite arbitral proceedings, institutions set deadlines for delivering the award. The ICC aims at ensuing that arbitral tribunals render the final award within six months from the date of the last signature by the parties or the arbitrators of the Terms of Reference.[43] How practical these timetables are in real terms is debatable, as deadlines depend not only on the times agreed or fixed for the presentation of the case but also on all concerned, including the parties and their lawyers, keeping to the agreed timetable, as well as other external factors. Sometimes there are too many issues to determine, but the tribunal nonetheless has to deal with them to avoid an *infra petita* argument.

d. Duty to keep the arbitration confidential

Are arbitrators bound by a duty of confidentiality in international arbitration?[44] It is suggested that this duty arises as "a prerogative inherent in [the arbitrators'] judicial function".[45] The confidentiality obligation also has a contractual nature, arising from the arbitration agreement or, indirectly, through the application of arbitral rules.[46] Some institutions can also require arbitrators to enter into explicit declarations of confidentiality.[47] Depending on the circumstances, other sources include regulations of the professional bodies to which the arbitrator belongs and ethical guidelines such as the AAA/ABA Code of Ethics for Arbitrators in Commercial Disputes[48] and the IBA Rules of Ethics for International Arbitrators.[49]

Deliberations are generally confidential and should not be disclosed. The principle of confidential deliberations goes to the heart of the arbitrators' independent adjudicatory role.[50] Arbitrators are often discouraged from publishing dissenting opinions in the award. However, in certain instances, arbitrators have been called before courts to provide testimony about past arbitrations.[51]

The extent of this duty is unclear. Does it cover the existence of the arbitration, the subject matter, the names of the parties or the legal issues? A more complicated question is whether this duty of confidentiality requires arbitrators not to disclose information about money laundering transactions and transnational criminality to the relevant authorities. It is suggested that the tension between the arbitrators' confidentiality obligations and the public interest duty to report illegalities must be approached from a jurisdictional perspective. This will require a tribunal to carefully consider how to deal with a case when it suspects that the dispute is a sham or that the underlying transaction involves criminal behaviour.[52] The arbitrator should not turn a blind eye and issue an award in accordance with the parties' wishes. Yet, under the current state of law, it is not clear whether the arbitrators have a duty to report suspicious behaviour. This question remains to be dealt with at national level.

e. Duty to deliver an enforceable award

Is it realistic or even feasible to expect arbitrators to deliver awards conforming to local laws and foresee all places where recognition and enforcement are sought? Thomas Clay argues that arbitrators can achieve this goal at three levels: first, by "improving the award" by completing gaps, clarifying vague points and correcting errors; second, by participating in enforcement procedures, such as in Belgium where arbitrators are required to register the awards with the legal authorities;[53] and, third, by being involved in the setting-aside procedure.[54] Supporting examples come from Switzerland, where arbitrators may be called by the Federal Tribunal in post-arbitration litigation, and from Norway and Thailand, where arbitrators have been called to give explanations in court regarding the discussions between the parties and the award.[55]

Assuming that the duty to deliver enforceable awards exists, to what extent are arbitrators willing and able to complete such a duty after the arbitration ends? Is testifying about the arbitration implied in the arbitrator's contract with the parties? Who pays for the expenses associated with such testimony once the tribunal is *functus officio*? Would it be fair to ask the arbitrators to cover the costs associated with such testimony? Should they factor them into their contract with the parties? These questions await debate and call for pragmatic answers.

4. ARBITRATOR'S RIGHTS

Arbitrator's rights are not widely discussed, especially in contrast to the discussion of arbitrators' obligations. When considering arbitrators' rights, it is essential to differentiate between the rights and powers (or authority) of the tribunal. Since arbitrators have obligations, do they also have commensurate rights?

A right is "something that is due to a person by just claim, legal guarantee, or ethics" or "a legally enforceable claim that another will do or will not do a given act".[56] Power, on the other hand, is "the legal right or authorization to act or not to act; the ability conferred on a person by the law to alter, by an act of will, the rights, duties, liabilities, or other legal relations either of that person or of another".[57] In the arbitration context, we talk about the arbitrators' power to direct the parties and conduct the procedure in accordance with their mandate as defined by the arbitration agreement, the applicable rules or national law. It is suggested that arbitrators' rights under the present state of law include: the right to remuneration, the right to free decision making and, under certain circumstances, the right to resign.

a. Remuneration

Remuneration is the principal right of the arbitrator. For many, it may be the *raison d'être* for taking on the role of an arbitrator. In return for his services, the arbitrator receives remuneration by way of fees. The right to remuneration stems either from the agreement with the parties, the arbitration rules or the applicable law. The costs of the arbitration—or at least how they are to be made up—should be clear and understood from the outset. Arbitrators' fees may be calculated based on the time spent (hourly or daily rates) or on the amount in dispute (the *ad valorem* system). Even when there is no agreement on fees, it is accepted that "an arbitrator appointed to decide a commercial dispute has a right to be paid a reasonable fee".[58]

However, a key practical issue, specifically for *ad hoc* arbitrations, is that the arbitrators' remuneration should be agreed on appointment or very soon after. This may include hourly and daily rates, travel time and cancellation fees (where a hearing is postponed or cancelled within a specified time before a scheduled hearing). Arbitrators and parties should also deal with reimbursement of expenses incurred for the purpose of the arbitration (e.g., travel, couriers and hotels) and periodic billing. There is no reason why an arbitrator should wait until the case is completed before being paid for work undertaken.

Typically, parties are jointly and severally liable for the arbitrator's remuneration. The English Arbitration Act provides that the parties are jointly and severally liable to pay to the arbitrators "such reasonable fees and expenses (if any) as are appropriate in the circumstances".[59] When one party agrees to fix rates of remuneration while the other consents to reasonable fees, joint and several liability applies only to the reasonable amount. In principle, this can be lower or higher than the agreed fee. "[I]n practice, the agreed fee is likely to be the same as or accepted to be a reasonable fee."[60]

A more delicate issue is dealing with the arbitrators' remedies in case of non-payment. Can the arbitrators stop the proceedings or refuse to release the award if parties do not make the agreed/necessary payment? Alternatively, if the fees prove insufficient during the proceedings, can the arbitrators approach the parties for an augmentation? Can either party pay the shortfall of deposits requested? These issues should be addressed in the arbitrator's contract either directly or through the applicable rules or law.

b. Immunity from suit

It is generally recognized that arbitrators enjoy immunity from suit. This protects arbitrators from being blamed, harassed, pressured, threatened or blackmailed by the dissatisfied parties. Ultimately, immunity is meant to encourage an independent and impartial decision-making process.

The existence and extent of immunity will depend on the applicable national law or arbitration rules. It can also be dealt with in the arbitrator's terms of appointment. Through their agreement, parties can limit arbitrators' immunity, albeit such instances are rarely reported in practice.[61] Without immunity, arbitrators would arguably be reluctant to take cases and fulfil their mandate.

Some arbitration rules promote complete immunity for arbitrators. For instance, article 40 of the ICC Arbitration Rules (2012) provides that arbitrators, any person appointed by the tribunal and the emergency arbitrator "shall not be liable to any person for any act or omission in connection with the arbitration, except to the extent that such limitation of liability is prohibited by applicable law". Article 31.1 of the LCIA Rules follows a narrower approach, allowing for the removal of immunity "where the act or omission is shown by that party to constitute conscious and deliberate wrongdoing committed by the body or person alleged to be liable to that party".

At national level, there is no uniform approach. Some laws are more protective than others, providing for arbitrators' liability only for acts or omissions in bad faith.[62] Others—typically the jurisdictions following the UNCITRAL Model Law— tend to be silent on this matter.[63]

c. The right to free decision making

In order to exercise their role and complete their mandate effectively, the arbitrators should be free of any external constraints and tensions. This includes: (a) the right to protection against vexatious conduct by parties or their representatives; (b) non-interference in decision making; and (c) the secrecy of deliberations.

I. PROTECTION AGAINST VEXATIOUS CONDUCT

Vexatious conduct can manifest itself in different ways: threats to the physical integrity of arbitrators or their family members, blackmail, offensive language in the correspondence copied to the tribunals and even kidnapping. Arbitrators have the right to carry out their mission free from pressure, intimidation and threat of physical and mental aggression from any arbitration participant or third party.

In the *Himpurna* arbitration involving Indonesia,[64] there were repeated attempts to intimidate the members of the tribunal. Professor Priyatna, the arbitrator nominated by the Indonesian government, was kidnapped from the airport en route to a deliberations meeting with the other arbitrators. The perpetrators hoped that Professor Priyatna's absence would preclude the other arbitrators from issuing an interim award and eventually force them to cancel the proceedings. Relying on Professor Priyatna's absence, government representatives also unsuccessfully challenged the arbitration before the Dutch courts. Despite these threats, the remaining arbitrators issued an interim award and recorded the reasons for the third arbitrator's absence. Professor Priyatna was subsequently released, but later on in the proceedings he and his co-arbitrators faced claims raised by the Indonesian Ministry of Finance before a local court in Jakarta to the effect that they would be fined USD 1 million per day if they continued with the arbitration. Fortunately, due to a change in the political regime, these claims were subsequently withdrawn. The arbitration eventually continued, but the kidnap remained as a disgraceful episode in the history of international arbitration.

Another example occurred during the ICSID proceedings in *Biwater Gauff (Tanzania) Ltd v. United Republic of Tanzania*.[65] An organization initiated a campaign to persuade Biwater to discontinue the ongoing ICSID arbitration. The organization reportedly set up a link on its website in an attempt to "exert personal pressure on claimant's chairman".[66] These attempts at intimidation made their way to the tribunal through a party application for provisional measures.

Over the years, various tribunals have held that parties' conduct should not prejudice the integrity of the arbitral procedure, nor aggravate or exacerbate the dispute.[67] This type of behaviour undermines the whole process but is fortunately rare. It is important that arbitrators are not intimidated and are left free to reach their decision without fear or any other interference.

II. NON-INTERFERENCE IN THE DECISION-MAKING PROCESS

Parties generally expect a speedy dispute resolution. This goal is easier to achieve in some cases than in others. The reality is that cases are often more complicated than initially envisaged, and there are sometimes genuine reasons for last-minute drama and delays. Once the proceedings are closed, parties should abstain from interfering in the making of the award.

Parties should abstain from compromising the arbitration by seeking the arbitrators' presence or company at any type of private or public event or by sitting next to the arbitrator on plane, particularly during the deliberations stage. Parties should not send additional unsolicited submissions to the tribunal raising issues that they did not think of at an earlier time. While arbitrators will reject such submissions, inevitably the other party will feel it must have the right of reply. This behaviour is an unnecessary and invariably an unjustifiable distraction that interferes with the process.

III. SECRECY OF DELIBERATIONS AND THE RIGHT TO DISSENT

Secrecy of deliberations goes to the heart of the arbitrators' independent function and the private nature of arbitration. It lies at the cross-roads between a duty and a right. As a duty, it is an integral part of the arbitrators' obligation to maintain confidentiality over the proceedings. As a right, it affords arbitrators the protection needed for a free decision-making process. The positions taken and views expressed by arbitrators during deliberations and their exchanges in the making of the award should be confidential.

Secrecy of deliberations is not absolute. Parties may limit it through their express agreement or the circumstances may require disclosing parts of the decision-making process. For example, article 30.2 of the LCIA Rules provides: "The deliberations of the Arbitral Tribunal are likewise confidential to its members, save and to the extent that disclosure of an arbitrator's refusal to participate in the arbitration is required of the other members of the Arbitral Tribunal under Articles 10, 12 and 26." This provision calls for disclosure if an arbitrator dies, is seriously ill, refuses or becomes unable or unfit to act, acts in violation of the arbitration agreement, does not act fairly and impartially or fails to conduct the proceedings with reasonable diligence.

Courts may also limit the secrecy of deliberations. In *CME v. Czech Republic*,[68] for example, the Svea Court of Appeals held that the obligation to testify overrode the principle of confidentiality surrounding deliberations in arbitral proceedings. The court held that no penalties would be imposed but rather that negative inferences could be drawn from a failure to testify. Notwithstanding the court's permissive ruling, all three arbitrators testified.

Under certain rules, arbitrators can express opinions that depart from the majority's view. In these cases, one can speak of the arbitrators' right to express dissent. The right to secrecy of deliberations may be considerably limited where the dissenting opinions can be made public. For example, article 48(4) of the ICSID Convention provides: "Any member of the Tribunal may attach his individual opinion to the award, whether he dissents from the majority or not, or a statement of his dissent."[69] Similarly, article 32(3) of the Rules of Procedure of the Iran-United States Claims Tribunal reads:

> *"The arbitral tribunal shall state the reasons upon which the award is based, unless the parties have agreed that no reasons are to be given. Any arbitrator may request that his dissenting vote or his dissenting vote and the reasons therefor be recorded."*

d. The right to resign

An arbitrator cannot be forced to continue taking part in the proceedings against his will. For this reason, arbitrators should have the right to resign at any time during the proceedings, although their resignation may be seen as contradicting their general duty to complete their mandate.

Many laws significantly qualify or limit the right to resign. This is the practice in England, where arbitrators cannot resign absent a specific agreement with the parties.[70] Even so, the DAC Report recognizes that:

> *"[i]n theory it could be said that an arbitrator cannot unilaterally resign if this conflicts with the express or implied terms of his engagement. However, as a matter of practical politics an arbitrator who refuses to go on cannot be made to do so, though of course he may incur a liability for breach of his agreement to act."[71]*

Some laws recognize only resignation for cause;[72] others imply it in the arbitrator's failure or impossibility to act.[73] In other cases, the law requires arbitrators to obtain leave from the court before exercising their right to resign.[74]

When an arbitrator's decision to relinquish his function is made without cause or without the leave of a court where such a requirement exists, the arbitrator may be liable for damages or face a reduction in fees. If the right to resign is exercised in bad faith, so as to delay, hamper or scuttle the process, the other arbitrators may continue their mandate and decide without the resigning arbitrator.[75]

5. A FINAL WORD

In the light of the above analysis, one open question remains: ought there to be a corresponding right to every obligation? Such correspondence is not easy to find in international arbitration. However, if arbitrators are expected and required to act in certain ways, arbitrators naturally need to have the power and authority to take the necessary actions to achieve those expectations. Power and authority are based in the arbitrator's contract whether arising under contract, from the applicable institutional rules or from governing law. In addition to the arbitrators' rights discussed above, namely the right to remuneration, immunity from suit, the right to resign and the right to free decision making, it may be appropriate to recognize arbitrators' powers as a right rather than an authority. The origin of the rights will remain the same, namely the parties' agreement to arbitration. However, would it make the arbitral process stronger and increase its autonomy if it was accepted that arbitrators' rights mirrored the many obligations expected and required from and imposed on arbitrators?

Endnotes:

1   Gary Born, *International Commercial Arbitration* (2009) pp. 1595-1597.

2   Julian Lew, Loukas Mistelis and Stefan Kröll, *Comparative International Commercial Arbitration* (2003) p. 276.

3   Christian Hausmaninger, 'Rights and Obligations of the Arbitrator with Regard to the Parties and the Arbitral Institution—A Civil Law Viewpoint', in *ICC Court Bulletin—Special Supplement—The Status of the Arbitrator* (1995) p. 37 et seq.

4   In the Netherlands and Switzerland, the contract with the arbitrator is qualified as an agency agreement or a mixed contract with features similar to an agency contract. In this sense, see Jean-François Poudret and Sébastien Besson, *Comparative Law of International Arbitration* (2007) p. 368.

5   In Germany, the contract between the parties and the arbitrator is considered a contract for services. See Poudret and Besson, *supra* note 4, at p. 368; see also Emmanuel Gaillard and John Savage (eds.), *Fouchard, Gaillard, Goldman on International Commercial Arbitration* (1999) pp. 606-607, paras. 1119-1121.

6   Born, *supra* note 1, at 1607.

7   *Jivraj v. Hashwani* [2011] UKSC 40.

8   Id., at [40].

9   Id., at [41].

10   *ICT Pty Ltd v. Sea Containers Ltd* [2002] NSWC 77, [42].

11   *DAC Report on Arbitration Bill* (2006) ch. 2, para. 155, available at: <http://arbitration. practicallaw.com/5-205-4994#sect1pos2res1> (last visited 19 December 2011).

12   Id., at para 157.

13   Lew, Mistelis and Kröll, *supra* note 2, at p. 279.

14   Antonio Crivellaro, 'An Art, a Science or a Technique?', in Albert Jan van den Berg (ed.), *Arbitration Advocacy in Changing Times*, ICCA Congress Series no. 15 (2011) p. 9 at p. 16.

15   Limited document production is accepted and largely practiced in international arbitration. The IBA Rules on the Taking of Evidence in International Arbitration provide that document production requests should call for disclosure only of "documents in the possession, custody or control of the other party", "relevant to the case", and "material to its outcome". In this sense, see article 3(b) and (c) of the IBA Rules.

16   See, e.g., Friederike Schäfer, 'Practical Problems Arising from the Contractual Relationship Between Expert and Participants in an Arbitration', in Christian Klausegger et al. (eds.), *Austrian Yearbook on International Arbitration* 11 (2011) pp. 113-127.

17   Kay Hobér, *International Commercial Arbitration in Sweden* (2011) p. 222 at paras. 6.101-6.102.

18   See, e.g., article 17 of the UNCITRAL Arbitration Rules (2010).

19   Julian Lew, 'Arbitrators' Control of Tactical and Procedural Issues in the 21 Century', in Ian Fletcher at al. (eds.), *Foundations and Perspectives of International Trade Law* (2001) pp. 248, 252.

20   Article 21(2) of the ICC Rules (2012); article 35.3 of the UNCITRAL Rules (2010).

21   See, e.g., Gabrielle Kaufmann-Kohler, 'Iura Novit Arbiter—Est-ce bien raisonnable? Réflexions sur le statut de droit du fond devant l'arbitre international', *in Réflexions sur le Droit Désirable en l'Honneur du Professeur Alain Hirsch* (2004) pp. 71-78; Lew, *supra* note 19, at pp. 253-254; See also Julian Lew, 'Iura Novit Curia and Due Process', in Yves Derains and Laurent Lévy (eds.), *Liber Amicorum en l'honneur de Serge Lazareff* (2011).

22   Born, *supra* note 1, at p. 1626.

23   In this sense, see Alexis Mourre, 'Arbitration and Criminal Law: Reflections on the Duties of the Arbitrator', *Arbitration International* 22(1) (2006) pp. 95-118. Alexis Mourre notes that "it is because arbitrators are the natural judges of international trade that they are the natural guardians of ethics and good morals in international commerce. They may even be better placed than national judges to combat international fraud." Id., at p. 96.

24   Thomas Clay, 'The Role of the Arbitrator in the Execution of the Award', *ICC Bulletin* 20(1) (2009) p. 43 at p. 45.

25   Cannon I (E) of the AAA/ABA Code of Ethics for Arbitrators in Commercial Disputes.

26   Lew, Mistelis and Kröll, *supra* note 2, at p. 280.

27   See *La Société Commercial Caribbean Niquel v. La Société Overseas Mining Investments Ltd*, Paris Court of Appeals, 1st Chamber, 08/23901, 25 March 2010. In this case, the award was annulled because the arbitrators raised a new legal theory in granting damages replacing that invoked by the requesting counsel. For a discussion of the case, see William Park, 'The Four Musketeers of Arbitral Duty: Neither One-For-All Nor All-For-One', *ICC Dossiers: Is Arbitration Only as Good as the Arbitrator? Status, Powers and Role of the Arbitrator*, ICC publication no. 714E (2011) p. 25 at pp. 28-29.

28   The will of George Washington is available at: <http://gwpapers.virginia.edu/documents/will/text.html> (last visited 5 January 2012).

29   LCIA reference no. 81160 (29 August 2009), *Arbitration International* 27(3) (2011) p. 442 at p. 449, para. 3.5; LCIA reference no. 81224 (15 March 2010), *Arbitration International* 27(3) (2011) p. 461 at pp. 465-466, paras 3.2-3.6.

30   Lew, Mistelis and Kröll, *supra* note 2, at p. 258.

31   Born, supra note 1, at pp. 1475-1476.

32   Thomas Walsh and Ruth Teitelbaum, 'The LCIA Court Decisions on Challenges to Arbitrators: An Introduction', *Arbitration International* 27(3) (2011) p. 283 at p. 287. See also LCIA reference no. 81160, supra note 29, at p. 449, para. 3.8; LCIA reference no. 81224, *supra* note 29, at p. 466, para. 3.7.

33   Walsh and Teitelbaum, supra note 32, at pp. 287-288. See also LCIA reference no. 81160, *supra* note 29, at p. 449, para. 3.9; LCIA reference no. 81224, *supra* note 29, at p. 466, para. 3.8.

34   Walsh and Teitelbaum, supra note 32, at p. 288.

35   *Universal Compression International Holdings, S.L.U. v. The Bolivarian Republic of Venezuela*, ICSID case no. ARB/10/09, Decision on the Proposal to Disqualify Prof. Brigitte Stern and Prof. Guido Santiago Tawil, para. 92, available at: <http://icsid.worldbank.org/ICSID/FrontServlet?requestType=CasesRH&actionVal=showDoc&docId=DC2411_En&caseId=C1021> (last visited 5 January 2012).

36   See, e.g., General Standard 3(c) of the IBA Guidelines on Conflicts of Interest in International Arbitration.

37   *J&P Avax SA v. Tecnimont SPA*, Cour d'appel de Paris, 1st chamber (section C), 12 February 2009, case no. 07/22164. The Paris Court of Appeal annulled an ICC award on the grounds that the chairman, despite disclosing a conflict of interest upon nomination, failed to update his disclosure statement. Upon nomination, the chairman stated that his law firm provided assistance to the respondent's parent company, but that the case was closed and, moreover, that he never worked on any matter for that client. While the arbitration was pending, the appellant continued questioning the chairman's law firm's relationship with the respondent. Almost five years into the arbitration, the chairman disclosed that, while the arbitration was pending, certain offices of his law firm represented the respondent's parent company and

advised two subsidiaries and that one colleague attorney was appointed sole arbitrator in a dispute involving one of respondent's subsidiaries. After unsuccessfully challenging the appointment before the ICC, the appellant continued to participate in the arbitration under protest. Shortly after a partial award was issued, the chairman resigned for reasons related to his perceived incompatibility. The partial award was ultimately annulled by the Court of Appeals for the chairman's failure to disclose conflicts of interest between offices of his law firm and the respondent's corporate group.

38   Article 18 of the UNCITRAL Model Law on International Commercial Arbitration.

39   Section 33(1) of the English Arbitration Act 1996.

40   Section 10 of the Federal Arbitration Act.

41   Article V.1(b) of the Convention on the Recognition and Enforcement of Foreign Arbitral Awards.

42   Lew, Mistelis and Kröll, *supra* note 2, at p. 282.

43   Article 30(1) of the ICC Arbitration Rules (2012).

44   Julian Lew, 'The Arbitrator and Confidentiality', in *ICC Dossiers: Is Arbitration Only as Good as the Arbitrator? Status, Powers and Role of the Arbitrator*, ICC Publication No. 714E (2011) pp. 105-129; See also Gaillard and Savage, *supra* note 5, at p. 612, para. 1132; Born, *supra* note 1, at p. 1631 et seq.; Poudret and Besson, *supra* note 5, at p. 320; Lew, Mistelis and Kröll, *supra* note 2, at p. 283.

45   Gaillard and Savage, *supra* note 5, at pp. 627-628, para. 1167.

46   See, e.g., article 34 of the AAA International Rules, article 18 of the ACICA Rules, article 8 of the Arbitration Rules of the Chamber of National and International Arbitration of Milan, article 7 of the Rules of Arbitration of the Court of International Commercial Arbitration attached to the Chamber of Commerce and Industry of Romania, article 37 of the CIETAC Rules, article 36 of the CAMCA Arbitration Rules, rule 9 of the KLRCA Rules, article 30 of the LCIA Arbitration Rules, article 43 of the Swiss Rules of International Arbitration, and article 76 of the WIPO Arbitration Rules.

47   Rule 6(2) of the ICSID Arbitration Rules provides: "I shall keep confidential all information coming to my knowledge as a result of my participation in this proceeding, as well as the contents of any award made by the Tribunal."

48   Cannon VI of the AAA/ABA Code of Ethics for Arbitrators in Commercial Disputes.

49   Article 9 (Confidentiality of the Deliberations) of the IBA Rules of Ethics for International Arbitrators.

50   *Himpurna California Energy Ltd. v. Republic of Indonesia*, Interim Ad Hoc Award, 26 September 1999, in A.J. van den Berg (ed.), Yearbook Commercial Arbitration XXV (2000) pp. 112, 151.

51   *CME v. Czech Republic*, Svea Court of Appeal, Sweden, case no. T8735-01, 15 May 2003, available at: <http://www.chamber.se/filearchive/2/21294/CME_tjeckiska_republiken.pdf> (last visited 5 January 2012); *Mond & Mond v. Dayan Rabbi Isaac Dov Berger* [2004] VSC 45.

52   Lew, *supra* note 44, at p. 123.

53   Article 1702(2) of the Belgian Judicial Code reads: "The chairman of the arbitral tribunal shall deposit the original of the award with the registry of the Court of First Instance; he shall notify the parties of the deposit."

54   Clay, *supra* note 24, at p. 47.

55   Id., at 48.

56   Bryan Garner, *Black's Law Dictionary*, 7th ed. (1999) p. 1322.

57   Id., at p. 1189.

58   *Mustill & Boyd: Commercial Arbitration*, 2nd ed. (2001) at p. 223. See also *K/S Norjarl AS v. Hyundai Heavy Industries Co Ltd* [1991] 1 Lloyd's Rep. 524.

59   Section 28 of the Arbitration Act 1996.

60   at *Linnett v. Halliwells LLP* [2009] EWHC 319, at para. 62.

61   Lew, Mistelis and Kröll, *supra* note 2, at p. 290.

62   See, e.g., section 29 of the Arbitration Act 1996.

63   Lew, Mistelis and Kröll, supra note 2, at p. 292.

64   H. Priyatna Abdurrasyid, 'They Said I Was Going to Be Kidnapped', *Mealey's International Arbitration Report* 18(6) (2003) p. 29 at p. 31.

65   Biwater Gauff Tanzania Ltd. v. United Republic of Tanzania, ICSID case no. ARB/05/22, Procedural Order no. 3, available at: <http://icsid.worldbank.org/ICSID/FrontServlet?requestType=CasesRH&actionVal=showDoc&docId=DC1583_En&caseId=C67> (last visited 5 January 2012).

66   Id., at para. 16.

67   See, e.g., *Amco Asia Corp., US and others v. Republic of Indonesia*, ICSID case no. ARB/81/1, Decision on Request for Provisional Measures of 9 December 1983, in A.J. van den Berg (ed.), *Yearbook Commercial Arbitration* XI (1986) pp. 159-161; *Biwater Gauff (Tanzania) Ltd v. United Republic of Tanzania*, supra note 65, at p. 34, para. 135 et seq.

68   Svea Court of Appeal, Sweden, case no. T8735-01, 15 May 2003, available at: <http://www.chamber.se/filearchive/2/21294/CME_tjeckiska_republiken.pdf> (last visited 5 January 2012).

69   In the same vein, rule 46 of the ICSID Arbitration Rules provides: "The award (including any individual or dissenting opinion) shall be drawn up and signed within 120 days after closure of the proceeding."

70   See Article 2 of the Arbitration Act 1996.

71   *DAC Report on Arbitration Bill* (2006) clause 25.

72   Article 1457(1) of French Decree no. 2011-48 of 13 January 2011.

73   Section 1038 of the German Arbitration Act 1998 (Book 10 ZPO).

74   See article 1689 of the Belgian Judicial Code of 19 May 1998 and article 1029 of the Dutch Arbitration Act of 1 December 1986, Code of Civil Procedure—Book Four: Arbitration.

75   Poudret and Besson, *supra* note 4, at p. 657, para. 738; Pierre Lalive, 'Du nouveau sur les tribunaux arbitraux "tronqués"?', *ASA Bulletin* 2 (1999) pp. 211-219; Jean-Pierre Ancel, 'Measures Against Dilatory Tactics: The Cooperation Between Arbitrators and the Courts', in Albert Jan van den Berg (ed.), *Improving the Efficiency of Arbitration Agreements and Awards*, ICCA Congress Series no. 9 (1999) p. 410 at pp. 418-419; Nigel Blackaby et al., *Redfern and Hunter on International Arbitration*, 5th ed. (2009) p. 288, paras. 4.141-4.142.

CHAPTER SIX

THE CHAIRMAN'S ROLE IN THE ARBITRAL TRIBUNAL'S DYNAMICS

Laurent Lévy

1. INTRODUCTION

The title of this paper, as suggested by the organizers of the 2011 Conference of the ICC Institute, refers to the "chairman" of the arbitral tribunal, but I nevertheless intend to use the word "president". There are many possible reasons for such a substitution. Suffice it to point to one, namely that this is also the term used in the new ICC Arbitration (and ADR) Rules, which entered into force on 1 January 2012.[1]

In fact, the ICC Rules, both in their previous and current versions, do not say much about the tribunal's president, beyond indicating how he is to be appointed (articles 12 and 13) and that he can, under certain circumstances, make an award by himself (article 31). In this, the ICC Rules are in no way an exception. Quite the contrary: most of the laws and rules on arbitration do not dwell much on the president or his role, other than providing a method for his appointment and, in some instances, granting him specific powers with respect to the making of awards or, more rarely, procedural orders. Likewise, in preparing this paper, I have come across only a handful of articles and studies devoted specifically to the president and his functions or powers.[2]

This may come as a surprise, given the importance of the brief and the role that the presidents of arbitral tribunals are called to assume in international arbitrations. Presidents have a "pivotal" role "in ensuring a smooth-running and fair arbitration"; they are, in a sense, "the glue that holds the whole process together".[3] It is true that the president occupies a "special position"[4] within the tribunal: he is often the only arbitrator whom neither party has directly appointed and is thus endowed with a "particular aura of independence".[5] Being in charge of the conduct of the proceedings, he will be more involved in the arbitration process than his colleagues; he will interact with each of his co-arbitrators (or preferably with both of them together) and be the one point of contact or, to use a fashionable yet very fitting term, the interface between the tribunal, the parties and, where relevant, the arbitral institution that administers the proceedings.

Yet, it is just as evident that, as a matter of positive law, the president is cloaked with little formal authority in discharging all these responsibilities. In reality, he will have to "acquire" such authority and seek, elicit and secure the cooperation of the parties (and/or their counsel), as well as the support of his colleagues in the tribunal, using his experience, his qualities and his personality. All this is necessary for the president to steer the arbitration proceedings, fairly and efficiently, all the way to their conclusion, allowing the tribunal to fully achieve its mandate, while successfully accomplishing his own mission in this regard.[6]

As a consequence, the normative framework (see section 2) may be less important than the manner in which the president chooses to put his powers to use in practice (see section 3). To a great extent, this fact may result from a misunderstanding, namely that the president is a person vested with formal authority and power over others. In reality, he is, first and foremost, merely an individual tasked with the function (and the responsibility) of conducting a procedure.[7]

2. THE NORMATIVE FRAMEWORK—WHAT DO THE RULES SAY (OR IMPLY)?

If the parties choose to have a three-member panel, the principle is that the arbitrators will jointly discharge their mandate. In other words, they will make their decisions together and collectively tend to the evidentiary proceedings, in particular by attending the hearing as a full tribunal.[8]

However, this is not to say that the president would be left without any additional prerogatives (see section 2.a)) or that there is no possibility for certain powers to be delegated to him (see section 2.b).

a. The president's implied powers

Case management (*direction de la procédure*) is an implied power of the president, subject to keeping the co-arbitrators informed and making sure they have no objections to his decisions in this context. This power derives from the arbitrators' general obligation to do the necessary to deliver an efficacious award within a reasonable time period, while keeping the costs of the arbitration under control. As long as the president does the job efficiently and without trespassing on the powers reserved for the full panel, this will be advantageous to all and is in fact the norm. As mentioned above, in most cases, the president is more regularly present and active in the arbitration—particularly with regard to its organizational and administrative aspects—than his two colleagues, who will generally rely on him as far as the day-to-day conduct of the proceedings is concerned. This is certainly the best practice, at least in the vast majority of arbitrations, namely all those where there is no intent to disrupt the proceedings—especially no arbitrator with a hidden agenda.

Such powers arise from the very nature of the presidential function, but also from the fact that there is a (sometimes simply practical) need for one member of a "composite" decisional body to represent it. This being so, the co-arbitrators should not be permitted to deprive their president of his prerogatives, like monitoring and conducting the proceedings or chairing the hearings. One reason for this is that there is, in principle, no contractual relationship among the arbitrators. Subject to any specific agreements regarding the splitting of their costs and/or fees, the arbitrators' relationship is procedural in nature, meaning that they must abide by the procedural rules applicable by virtue of the parties' agreement, including the definition and delimitation of the president's powers. At this juncture, it may be worth pointing out that such powers do not, as a matter of principle, go as far as to include the possibility for the president to actually give orders to his colleagues.[9]

I. OUTSIDE THE HEARINGS

- DISPOSING OF HEARING-RELATED MATTERS

The president has the power to set the place of the hearings, invite the parties to such hearings and determine their programme, exact times, duration and so forth. On these issues, consultation with his colleagues is absolutely indispensable,[10] among other reasons to ensure their availability. Consultation with counsel is also necessary in order to ascertain their and the parties' availability and to ensure the smooth running of the arbitration. However, if necessary, the president (or the full tribunal) may impose on the parties a certain date and/or place for the hearings.

- CONTACTS WITH THE PARTIES

The co-arbitrators should at all times refrain from having individual contacts with the parties, while the president may have some contact with both parties together. These contacts can take place via telephone calls, at conferences or in procedural hearings. They will sustain the momentum of the proceedings and may help avoid or clear misunderstandings. For instance, the president will be available to elucidate any questions relating to orders issued by the tribunal, resolve procedural differences between the parties or provide an interpretation of some rule of procedure. However, the president should always reserve the possibility for the co-arbitrators to be (collectively) involved in such contacts. It may be opportune to outline this approach in an initial letter to the parties, a copy of which will of course go to the co-arbitrators, expressly indicating that the arbitrators, including the president, will not have any ex parte contacts with either party. Urgency is an exception but arises less and less frequently in practice, as it usually suffices to address an e-mail (with a copy to the other party), for instance to request the extension of a time limit or to obtain a decision on most other urgent matters. *Ex parte* contacts are thus very rarely necessary.

- SETTING (OR AT LEAST AMENDING) TIME LIMITS

This has become so customary that there should be a recognized implied power of the president to this effect—provided, of course, that no contrary rules, especially statutory ones, apply.

- POWER TO SIGN THE TRIBUNAL'S PROCEDURAL ORDERS ALONE

Most often, this power is also the subject of agreed applicable procedural rules. Rules of this kind have become so commonplace that, even in their absence, the president is presumed to have such power. However, subject to an agreement to the contrary, even though the president has the power to sign the tribunal's procedural orders, this ought to be done after consultation with the two co-arbitrators as to the contents of the procedural order, that is to say, the decision itself.[11] There also seems to exist an implied power of the president to render procedural orders alone in case of urgency, with the possibility of revision by the tribunal if the circumstances warrant such revision.[12] The real difficulty here is the proper definition of urgency, as well as the need to balance it against the severity or importance of the measure ordered. For instance, the president may venture into rendering a procedural order on his own if there is an imperative need to keep to mandatory time limits or protect evidence from disappearing. But this power may be excluded when the applicable rules clearly require the three members of the panel to make any rulings together.[13]

II. DURING THE HEARINGS

Always with the benefit of the assistance and support of his co-arbitrators, the president will have his own *domaine réservé* and, under all circumstances, will be called to play a specific role during the hearings.

- REPRESENTING THE FULL TRIBUNAL

An example of an emerging implied power of the president (as opposed to a delegated power) is the increasing practice of having him represent the full tribunal at procedural hearings. This sometimes applies to the initial hearing but more often to the so-called "pre-hearing conference". Such appears to be the current trend, and it is usually already agreed upon at the earliest stage of the proceedings, albeit with the reservation that the co-arbitrators will be called if necessary. The pre-hearing conference will usually be held by telephone and will be devoted to procedural matters, limited to the administrative and organizational aspects of the hearing (e.g., sequence of witnesses, interpretation, allocation of time, etc.), but may sometimes also extend to the determination of actual procedural issues (e.g., whether or not to call certain witnesses, attendance at the hearing of certain persons, such as witnesses, when not examined, etc.).

- CHAIRING THE HEARINGS

As the ICSID Arbitration Rules state: "The President of the Tribunal shall conduct its hearings..."[14] This includes the so-called *police de l'audience*, which encompasses time management (including suspensions of the proceedings, imposing silence or, if worse comes to worst, expelling a participant). This power obviously also includes putting questions to the parties and the witnesses, bearing in mind that the president should not monopolize the tribunal's question time and should always endeavour to cater for the needs and preferences of both counsel and the parties (for instance, there is no doubt that the arbitrators have the authority to put questions at any time but the issue is rather to use it at the right time and in the right fashion).

III. WITH RESPECT TO THE DELIBERATIONS

Deliberations must take place, as collegial decisions are of the very essence of multi-member tribunals.[15] They represent key moments in the dynamics and internal workings of the arbitral tribunal. In this context, the role and powers of the president can be of considerable importance, especially when it comes to breaking a stalemate.

- POWER TO ORGANIZE THE DELIBERATIONS

The president is generally deemed to be responsible for structuring, coordinating and overseeing the tribunal's deliberations. Deliberations can take place in a single meeting or over the course of several meetings (or by other means, including correspondence) throughout the arbitration, in different contexts and with varying degrees of formality. The one fundamental rule that applies here is that the president must always keep both co-arbitrators informed. He should avoid unilateral contacts with one co-arbitrator and in any event should always immediately inform the other of such contacts, requesting his opinion. The president will usually define the procedure to be followed during the deliberations, including their timing (e.g., whether the first deliberation should take place at or right around the time of the evidentiary hearing or final oral submissions) and their format (e.g., questionnaires, identification of the issues, decisions by claims, etc.). In this context, the president should not fail to stress the confidentiality of the deliberation process (unless his colleagues are clearly familiar with that requirement). This is indispensable: a breach of the confidentiality of the deliberations may endanger the award itself as it may cause a breach of the parties' equality and right to be heard.[16]

- THE PRESIDENT'S CASTING VOTE

The following section examines the delegation of certain powers to the president. At this juncture, it should be stressed that the deliberations cannot be delegated to the president by the co-arbitrators. However, in this regard, a distinction must be made. No delegation will be allowed at all when it comes to reaching an opinion on an award proper, that is to say, the determination required of the tribunal on matters that go to its jurisdiction or the merits of the dispute (the tribunal's *pouvoirs juridictionnels*). Delegation may be possible for other decisions, such as procedural orders or even provisional measures, either by agreement of the parties or pursuant to statutory provisions.[17]

In as far as the deliberations on the award proper are concerned, in order to break a stalemate, the president may have a casting vote or even the power to decide alone, which is not, strictly speaking, a "delegation". These options are generally provided for in most statutes and arbitration rules.[18] In practice, it appears that this power is used very sparingly and that presiding arbitrators will usually manage to obtain a majority.[19] Robert Briner reported that, in the period between 2000 and 2008, there were only three instances of awards rendered by presidents deciding alone in ICC arbitrations.[20]

In fact, the normative framework should allow the president to have the necessary powers to advance the proceedings. However, as discussed below (see section 3), he should use such powers wisely and as sparingly as possible. Before examining these issues, it is important to consider the possibilities for proper delegations.

b. The delegation of powers to the president

As noted above, the delegation of tasks and powers to the president can be carried out either by the parties or by the arbitrators. The present discussion will be limited to the second alternative, since the first should not, in principle, give rise to particular difficulties (subject to any mandatory legal provisions prohibiting the delegation of certain powers).[21]

At any rate, it is clear that the arbitrators themselves may only delegate their responsibilities if the parties have not barred them from doing so. As seen above, there is no contractual relationship between the arbitrators, save for any specific agreements that they may conclude on the sharing of their fees or costs. As a result, unless there is a specific legal rule allowing delegation, the arbitrators' "agreement" to delegate is really just the exercise of a procedural discretion that the parties have, at least impliedly, vested in them. In order not to have to come back to this question, it should be pointed out here that the new ICC Rules do expressly insist on an expeditious and cost-effective conduct of the arbitration and refer to effective case management (article 22(1)-(2)). They also include an (updated) Appendix IV on Case Management Techniques, which provides examples of means to control time and costs. Whatever the reasons, there is no reference to the delegation of powers to the president as such a means or technique.[22]

What is expressly permitted or forbidden? As indicated, there is no possibility to delegate the power to decide on the case itself. The issue is whether it is permissible to delegate the conduct of the proceedings, especially the aspects related to time management and the taking of the evidence. There is little guidance to be found in the case law. The *Aranella* decision of the Paris Court of Appeal,[23] in particular, did hold that delegation could be allowed, if limited to specific tasks (e.g., site visits). *In casu*, the decision acknowledged that the president did not become privy to any information that was not accessible to his colleagues (through subsequent expert hearings and transcripts of the site visits conducted by the president). However, this case's precedential value is limited: its reasoning expressly turns on the consent of the parties, namely that they were aware of the delegation, did not object to it at the relevant time and that they should thus be understood to have consented to it.

I. TIME MANAGEMENT

The president may benefit from delegated powers with respect to the time management aspects of the arbitration (to the extent that this prerogative is not in part already vested in him as an implied power). He has the power to set and amend time limits. However, setting the procedural timetable itself is a matter that cannot be totally delegated, since: (1) it calls for the availability of all three arbitrators; and (2) it is linked to the shaping of the procedure itself, that is to say, its overall conduct (involving issues such as how many (rounds of) written submissions are to be made, the timing for the supply of the evidence, etc.). The tribunal may likewise delegate to the president the power to amend the procedural timetable, subject to the same restrictions (e.g., to consult with his colleagues if the amendment calls on their availability or represents an actual change in the shape of the procedure, especially where a decision to stay, or to lift a stay of the proceedings is at issue).

II. TAKING OF THE EVIDENCE

The arbitral tribunal shall itself take the evidence. This rule appears in certain statutes, like the Swiss PILA, which states in its article 184 that "[t]he Arbitral Tribunal shall itself conduct the taking of evidence".[24] Is it possible to derogate from this general rule? The PILA does not provide for derogations, and it is generally admitted that, as a result, no delegation is possible (without the parties' consent).[25] Other laws, such as the Italian Code of Civil Procedure, allow for the taking of the evidence to be delegated by the tribunal to the presiding arbitrator (or another member of the panel) without particular restrictions.[26] The French Code of Civil Procedure now expressly permits the delegation of the steps concerning evidentiary and procedural matters, including in international arbitrations, but only if the parties allow it.[27] Hence, it is possible for the arbitral tribunal to delegate a given evidentiary step (such as examining a witness or attending a site visit, including in the company of experts) to the president. It is true that this would deprive his co-arbitrators of the immediate "perception" of the evidence that only physical attendance can provide (such as remembering the attitude of a witness in order to assess his credibility), but this may be balanced against other factors (such as the possible urgency of hearing a witness or visiting a certain site, or cost-efficiency). At any rate, it is unlikely that a purported violation of the principle of collegiality in this respect would endanger the award. First, because the discontented party must object immediately, but also because such a violation would not normally result in a breach of due process or the equality of the parties. Second, this situation is not unlike the one that arises when an arbitrator is replaced during the proceedings. His successor will not have direct knowledge of the procedural and evidentiary steps carried out before his appointment but said evidentiary steps do not have to be repeated, at least not as a necessary consequence.[28]

Whatever the case may be, is it acceptable for the tribunal to decide that the president will perform all the steps in the evidentiary proceedings by himself without the parties' consent? The answer to this question is usually negative,[29] but there does not appear to be any real reason to distinguish between the two situations (partial or total delegation of activities relating to the taking of the evidence).[30] Such delegation should therefore be possible, subject of course to the parties' right to object. In all such cases, it is obviously appropriate for the arbitrators to advise the parties in advance, in order to give them a reasonable opportunity to make their positions known. This last *caveat* concerns the manner in which the president's powers are exercised, which forms the subject of the following section.

3. THE USE OF THE PRESIDENT'S POWERS

In principle, the president will be more actively involved in the proceedings than his two co-arbitrators, in particular by being responsible for the day-to-day monitoring and administrative "follow-up" activities on behalf of the full panel. His colleagues will normally rely on him in this regard. Thus, there is an implied duty for the president to see to it that the arbitral tribunal actually discharges its obligations during the whole course of the proceedings (be it by delegation or otherwise). That being said, it is comforting for the president when one or both of the co-arbitrators support him in this regard, for instance by drawing his attention to the need or opportunity to do something at any given time.

The president must at all times remember that the tribunal is entrusted with a single core duty, namely to resolve the dispute. Other obligations (e.g., cost-efficiency or sound and efficient time management) are not to be disregarded but are ancillary to this main duty, and their import tends to vary from one arbitration to the other. Thus, the president must focus on this main objective and, by his conduct, make his awareness of that objective *known to all*—the parties and their counsel, his co-arbitrators and, where relevant, the arbitral institution.

Being focused is one of the salient traits of a leader, that is, someone who is able to set goals, communicate them to others and marshal the necessary support for their realization. However, the president will have to adjust to the circumstances. He should tailor and fine-tune his own "style" of procedure to the specifics and evolution of the arbitration at hand. First and foremost, however, he should carefully evaluate who he going is to work with, especially to determine, as early as possible, (1) whether the parties are going to act in good faith towards the resolution of their dispute or whether one of them will likely endeavour to derail it; and (2) whether one or both of his co-arbitrators will cooperate or, to the contrary, adopt a partisan approach.[31] This is in fact essential, since, as seen above, the president has little power of coercion over the parties and none over his colleagues. He can give "orders" to the parties on behalf of the tribunal but should manage this commodity as sparingly as possible to avoid any wear and tear or even the risk of confronting a party or its counsel. To illustrate the point, the axiom here is that a good question will more often than not be preferable to an outright order.

a. The president and the parties

The president should make the parties aware that he has some authority and that he is willing to use it. The question is how and in what circumstances, while never forgetting that the president is not a sole arbitrator but rather the first among his colleagues and equals, the two co-arbitrators. The tribunal's brief is a joint brief that the parties first agree upon among themselves and, subsequently, with the arbitrators.

As to timing, the president should identify any "crisis"—or at least potential watersheds—in the arbitration and adjust his conduct accordingly. Every arbitration will feature some episodes of paroxysm or crisis, for which the tribunal and especially the president should be prepared, as well as, thankfully, some periods of relative calm.

Whether, at any given point in time, the situation requires a close watch or a less hands-on approach, the president may wish to decide from the outset how he would like to be perceived by the parties and how he intends to go about discharging his (and the tribunal's) duties towards them. Being excessively autocratic or authoritarian during the whole process will usually lead to fast decisions, which is an advantage in itself, but these decisions may be less than well accepted, especially if their grounds are not crystal-clear. This may lead, in turn, to a loss of trust in the arbitral tribunal, misunderstandings and aggravation. The tribunal must have and show respect for the attorneys and their work. For instance, imposing extremely tight time limits (or systematically refusing to extend them) will not be satisfactory to counsel if they do not see a need for this. It will not enhance the expeditiousness of the proceedings if counsel subsequently need extensions or if they prove unable to deliver quality products, whether in the form of written submissions, evidence and/or performance at the hearings. In other words, the president should not confuse the expeditious conduct of the proceedings with their hurried completion, especially if, at the end of the day, the arbitrators need a long time to agree upon, draft and notify an award (which will likely be the case if the work of counsel has been rushed).[32]

A relaxed approach is probably warranted in normal circumstances, provided of course that counsel are experienced and the parties are acting in good faith. That being said, the president should be able to determine immediately whether this "free rein approach" should be suspended (or abandoned altogether) at any moment, for instance if a crisis arises. This is true during the hearings but also outside the hearings. To continue with the equestrian metaphor, the conduct of the president must evidence that he is holding the reins loose but still holding them, ready to tighten his grip instantly if necessary. This in turn calls for availability, determination and firmness.

All the previous remarks lead to the following question: what are the specific qualities required of the tribunal's president and how should he display them? The answer to this question applies to the president's conduct vis-à-vis the parties and their counsel, as noted above, but also to the way he acts towards his fellow tribunal members and, more generally, to the way he discharges his overall responsibilities in connection with the arbitration.

When it comes to the way in which he exercises his authority, the president should basically remain himself. In other words, he should make use of his intrinsic qualities and accept his shortcomings (especially if the appointing counsel and arbitrators already knew him well when they selected him, thus accepting both). Reading the various descriptions of the qualities required of a president is truly frightening, as it seems that he must have them all: authority, experience, charisma, technical competence, reputation, courteousness, self-control, self-esteem, courage and so on. Obviously, it does not hurt to have any (or all!) of these features, but it appears that conscientiousness (which calls for availability), openness to new experiences, the ability to communicate, patience and a capacity to adjust to the circumstances are sufficient if the president is and remains focused on his well-defined objectives.[33]

B. THE PRESIDENT AND HIS CO-ARBITRATORS

"He will learn how to handle his co-arbitrators. The dynamics within an arbitral tribunal are a fascinating aspect of international arbitration, the study of which is yet to be done. Here we have three arbitrators, coming possibly from different legal, cultural and geographical backgrounds, who may have never met before and who have immediately to form a functioning unit able to dispose of procedural and substantive issues. Two of these arbitrators will have been appointed by parties having opposite interests, and each one may have his own conception of how to behave towards his appointing party, towards the opposite party, towards his colleagues. How to handle his co-arbitrators, how to build up the internal cohesion of the arbitral tribunal while at the same time respecting his colleagues' differences and allowing their expression in an appropriate manner, and how to maximize the chances that, whatever the outcome of the case, both party-appointed arbitrators will come out with the satisfactory feeling of having made a substantial and appreciated contribution to the decision-making process—these are the challenges facing the chairman."[34]

Handling—a word Jacques Werner uses twice in this quotation—co-arbitrators should not be confused with manipulation and should be understood as interacting with them or perhaps at most "managing" them, which is exercising the leadership that the president's role calls for.

As with the parties, and even *a fortiori*, the president should avoid adopting an authoritarian approach or an excessively lax attitude towards his co-arbitrators. The "right" conduct will of course depend on the personality of the president and those of his colleagues (as well as the specificities of the given arbitration), but the goal is to build a team and foster cooperation within it.

It is essential for the president not to give the impression that he would prefer to work alone in an ivory tower or to ostracize one of his colleagues, especially if this colleague is more junior than the other or less experienced in international arbitration. After all, the parties have agreed that there will be three arbitrators, not only the president. The latter therefore has to find the right balance to create and nurture a certain team spirit within the tribunal. In a nutshell, he will wish to make his fellow arbitrators feel that they are members of a united panel in which each member is expected to contribute to the achievement of the common goal—and thus never forget what that common goal is, namely resolving the dispute.

This does not mean that the president should ignore a colleague's request for assistance, for instance because he is less experienced in arbitration. More generally, it is not unusual for arbitrators to ask for guidance, for example as to when it would be advisable to study the submissions and the attached evidence (e.g., at the time of their receipt or subsequently). The president should always provide such guidance, while keeping the other arbitrator informed and eliciting his comments if that should be necessary. Likewise, advising the co-arbitrators with as much advance notice as possible that he will need their assistance is a good way for the president to nurture team spirit. He may thus implicitly coordinate the learning curves of the panel members and ascertain that both his colleagues will be available at the right time to supply their input. For instance, it is useful for the president to let the co-arbitrators know how he intends to deal with requests for document production orders, that is to say, whether he intends to ask their opinions before submitting a draft order to them or whether he intends to prepare a draft and then ask for their comments on it. In both instances letting them be prepared in time for their task. The same issue will arise, *a fortiori,* when the time comes for the deliberation and drafting of the award (see below).

A visibly united panel will also have an effect on counsel and the parties, who will usually take stock, be comforted and conduct themselves accordingly, for instance by not counting on either co-arbitrator to support any counter-productive motion, which in turn will be beneficial for the arbitration process as a whole.

This is not to say that all of the tribunal's decisions have to be taken unanimously. Unanimous decisions may be more easily accepted by the parties and also more readily enforced. Nevertheless, the president must be prepared to accept that unanimity is not always possible, be it for good reasons (such as serious differences of opinion, especially on legal matters) or bad ones. In fact, looking for unanimity *at all costs* may be detrimental.[35] First, what matters and what the president will seek is not unanimity but a collective decision—a decision that may perhaps dissatisfy one arbitrator but that is the result of an actual debate within the tribunal. A unanimous decision may appear to be satisfactory at first but can eventually prove unsatisfactory for all three arbitrators if it is not the end product of actual concert but rather the result of overstretched compromises and concessions. Second, and possibly worse, unanimous decisions may be achieved when the three arbitrators strive for unanimity at all costs, failing to consider alternative possibilities out of fear of breaking an apparent consensus, or, worse still, when one, possibly two or even all three arbitrators believe that the other two arbitrators have such convincing arguments that they should not (or no longer) express their own views on a given issue. Nothing endangers the decision-making process more than an arbitrator deciding to withhold his opinion in order not to appear to be breaking unanimity. If dissent is hidden, the arbitrators are not doing their job, and grudges will often surface later in the process, exacerbated by the passage of time.

It is the president's responsibility (at least chiefly) to identify such risks and prevent their realization. In order to do so, the president must not only evince impartiality, but also exercise the leadership his role calls for in a conspicuously impartial way. For instance, if one of the co-arbitrators is more formidable, experienced or prestigious than the other, the president may wish to invite the latter to express his views first. It is also important for the president always to reflect on the right time to express his own opinion. Once it is out, it will not be possible to withdraw it easily, and the two co-arbitrators will react and take a stance commenting on it, objecting to it, accepting it reluctantly or enthusiastically and so forth. At any rate, the president should not take silence for consent if he feels that such silence may be coerced. This also applies to the president himself, who may prefer to overcome his self-restraint and opine first if he fears that his colleagues will otherwise put so much pressure on him that he will not dare speak his own views.[36] Another possibility is for an arbitrator to say that he is playing "devil's advocate". It is telling that this is a frequently heard excuse for reluctantly expressing one's inner feelings in contradiction to the majority's view and it should thus be a red light for the president that may signal the uneasiness or reluctance of an arbitrator. The flip side is that the president may also wish to ask one of his colleagues to play devil's advocate in order to test an ostensibly agreed-upon proposition and its actual acceptance by each member of the tribunal. If the president becomes aware of instances of "self-censorship" by a co-arbitrator, provided this awareness does not arise very late in the process, he may wish to reopen discussions on previously agreed propositions, while making sure that he does not antagonize either of his two colleagues in the process. There are courteous and efficient ways of doing so, such as expressing regret for not having thought of the matter earlier or pointing to some passages or elements in the parties' submissions or in the evidence that the tribunal may not yet have (sufficiently) taken into account.

The same applies even if the president has a feeling that one of his colleagues is less than impartial, provided there are no suspicions that some information may be clandestinely communicated to one of the parties. Even a biased arbitrator may be helpful, in particular if he possesses specialized knowledge of relevance to the arbitration, for instance if he is the one member of the tribunal who is the most familiar with the law governing the merits (or has special expertise in a relevant area of said law). If this arbitrator does raise objections, they may be legitimate and it will be important to address them. If they are not, he will have been part of the deliberation process, which is advantageous in many regards.[37]

As for the actual drafting of the award, the basic principle mentioned above, namely that the co-arbitrators should be informed in advance of how the president intends to proceed so that they may prepare in time, naturally also applies in this connection. The president will usually draft the award himself, submitting working drafts, questionnaires and so on to his colleagues. Dividing the drafting work is also possible, and the late Robert Briner, for example, recommended and practiced this method.[38] This is a difficult decision, which will very much depend on the circumstances, including any specific expertise of the co-arbitrators. A good example is that of construction arbitrations, where it may be efficient to have a co-arbitrator draft the more technical sections of the award, such as those relating to quantification, if he is especially experienced in this area, for instance because he is an engineer by training. There are two caveats to this. First, synchronizing the work during the drafting and subsequent editing of the various parts of the award in order to produce a logical and coherent final text is a heavy and time-consuming task. Second, such "split" drafting should not impair the deliberation itself, namely by resulting in one arbitrator taking full responsibility for his part of the award, without actual control by the others. Thus, if there are successive drafts and/or rounds of deliberations, it will be useful to identify each time what has been agreed and finally deliberated as well as what remains to be decided. The redlining of "travelling drafts", possibly accompanied by a checklist or table of open items, is often a good way of doing this.

If the president has doubts about the integrity of one of his colleagues or feels that a stalemate is looming in the deliberation and drafting process, he may take the additional precaution of asking his co-arbitrators for their express confirmation that he has correctly reproduced the tribunal's decisions in the draft as it stands or ask for any suggestions that either of them might have at that juncture.[39] If an arbitrator fails to participate in the deliberation and drafting of the award in spite of invitations and reminders to this effect, the president will have no alternative but to continue the deliberation process by carrying on the exchange of further drafts with both his colleagues, thus always keeping the "absent" arbitrator fully informed. Likewise, the president will have to show courage and good time management if he eventually resorts to rendering the award by himself, or even mentions this possibility to his colleagues.[40] Before suggesting this extreme solution, which should always be reserved as a last resort, the president would be well advised to explore all possible avenues to keep the deliberation process from completely derailing. For instance, in an ICC arbitration, if possible in the circumstances of the case, this would be the time to close the proceedings. From that moment onwards, if an arbitrator "absconds", the ICC Court will have the power to allow the continuation of the arbitration with a truncated panel, without replacing the defaulting arbitrator.[41]

Similar questions arise if the president delegates some of his tasks to an assistant or to the secretary of the tribunal. This situation is examined in detail in Constantine Partasides' contribution to this dossier.

For present purposes, it is important to underscore again that the arbitrators—the president included—may not delegate their deliberation, that is to say, the forming of their decisions. Concretely, arbitrators should in general not commission a third person to draft texts pertaining to the essence of a decision without first having made that decision and, thus, giving directions as to the end result and, usually, the reasons that intimately support that result. But this is the sole limit on delegation. Arbitration has evolved: confronted with large teams of lawyers on each side and massive dockets, including hundreds of exhibits and authorities, the arbitrators and especially the president will, in order to be more efficient, have to delegate certain tasks and organize their activities and the tribunal's work accordingly. Although it has elicited severe criticism, the trend appears to be moving towards this sort of delegation. Arguing that it may tamper with the quality of the drafting does not seem warranted: an assistant may be more literate than the president of the tribunal, especially if the former is a born speaker of the arbitration's language and the latter is not. The exact limit in this regard may be difficult to establish. It is often said that writing will expose many issues that have gone unnoticed or even call into question decisions that had been made. While this may be so in some cases, the observation should not be generalized. After all, the same could be said of the other tasks that arbitrators perform, be it legal research or studying the evidence. Some presidents will be experts at team work and be able to manage assistants while fully preserving their ability to deliberate and decide, while others will not and will prefer to do everything themselves. Both systems work and neither is objectionable, provided there is always the required control.

In this area, as well as in those discussed earlier, the president's approach and methods in taking on and discharging his mandate will play a significant role, not only in the tribunal's dynamics but more generally in those of the arbitration itself.

Endnotes:

1   According to article 12(5) of the ICC Rules (2012), where the parties have agreed that their dispute will be referred to three arbitrators, the third arbitrator "will act as president of the arbitral tribunal".

2   Christian Gavalda, 'Le président du tribunal arbitral international', *Petites Affiches* No. 96, 25 May 1990, pp. 13-19; Claude Reymond, 'Le président du Tribunal arbitral', *Études offertes à Pierre Bellet* (Paris, 1991) pp. 467-482. The references to Claude Reymond's article in the following footnotes are to the French language version. The article was re-published in English a few years later in the ICSID Review: see Claude Reymond, 'The President of the Arbitral Tribunal', *ICSID Review* 9 (1994) p. 3 et seq.. More recently, see Neil Kaplan and Karen Mills, 'The Role of the Chair in International Commercial Arbitration', in M. Pryles and M. Moser, eds., *The Asian Leading Arbitrators' Guide to International Arbitration* (Huntington, 2007) pp. 119-163; Robert Briner, 'The Role of the President', in L.W. Newman and R.D. Hill, eds., *The Leading Arbitrators' Guide to International Arbitration*, 2nd ed. (Huntington, 2008) pp. 49-66.

3   Kaplan and Mills, *supra note* 2, at p. 119.

4   Gary Born, *International Commercial Arbitration* (Alphen aan de Rijn, 2009) p. 1663.

5   Peters Phillip, 'Presiding Arbitrator, Deciding Arbitrator: Decision-Making in Arbitral Tribunals', *Austrian Yearbook on International Arbitration* (2011) pp. 129-160 at p. 138.

6   About this distinction between the authority of the arbitrator as an inherent power and the "authority" arising from his "supériorité de mérite ou de séduction qui impose l'obéissance sans contrainte, le respect, la confiance" and the observation that "[c]'est en fait cette 'autorité' qui importe chez l'arbitre", see Antonias Dimolitsa, 'Sur "l'autorité" de l'arbitre', in Y. Derains and L. Lévy, eds., *Liber Amicorum en l'honneur de Serge Lazareff* (2011) pp. 207-211 *passim*, especially p. 208.

7   According to *Black's Law Dictionary*, a president is: "One placed in authority over others; a chief officer; a presiding or managing officer; a governor, ruler, or director. The chairman, moderator, or presiding officer of a legislative or deliberative body, appointed to keep order, manage the proceedings, and govern the administrative details of their business."

8   Dominique Hascher, 'Principes et pratique de procédure dans l'arbitrage commercial international', *Collected Courses of the Hague Academy of International Law* 279 (1999) p. 51 et seq., especially p. 141.

9   In fact, the way to grant additional powers, especially injunctive powers, to the president over his co-arbitrators is for the parties to agree to this prior to the appointment of the arbitrators or, with their unanimous consent, after their appointment. It does not appear that this form of agreement has ever occurred in a published award. It may be unrealistic to contemplate such a possibility, although it might be advantageous in some circumstances. For instance, if the president has the power to summon his colleagues to participate in deliberations or a hearing on a certain date or in a certain place, *a mala fide* arbitrator staying away will be in breach of such an order. He will of course also violate his general duty as an arbitrator to participate in the deliberations, but this may be more difficult to establish positively. However, such an agreement between the parties would have to be prudently drafted, and the president should be extremely cautious in exercising this power. To revisit the example of the order to participate in deliberations or a hearing, the president should certainly first consult his

colleagues about the time, place, opportunity and subject matter of such deliberations or such a hearing. Besides, what would be the sanction of the failure to obey a presidential order? Whatever the sanction might be, its enactment would destroy the homogeneity of the tribunal. This is an *ex absurdo* demonstration of the fact that the president is equal to his colleagues and should remain in this position.

10 See, however, rule 14(3) of the ICSID Rules, which provides that "[t]he President of the Tribunal shall fix the date and hour of its sittings" and could be interpreted to mean the contrary.

11 Some arbitration rules do expressly provide that the president may issue procedural orders alone if the parties or the arbitrators so agree. See, for instance, article 14(3) of the LCIA Rules, article 24(4) of the DIS Rules, article 31(2) of the Swiss Rules and article 33(2) of the UNCITRAL Rules.

12 The possibility of revision by the tribunal of orders on questions of procedure rendered by the presiding arbitrator alone is expressly provided for in article 33(2) of the UNCITRAL Rules and article 31(2) of the Swiss Rules.

13 See rule 16(1) of the ICSID Rules, providing that "[d]ecisions of the Tribunal shall be taken by a majority of the votes of all its members. Abstention shall count as a negative vote."

14 Rule 14(1) of the ICSID Rules. See also article R44.2 para 2 of the Code of Sports-related Arbitration and Mediation Rules (CAS Code): "The President of the Panel shall conduct the hearing and ensure that the statements made are concise and limited to the subject of the written presentations, to the extent that these presentations are relevant." Article 1693(2) of the Belgian Judicial Code provides that "[t]he chairman of the arbitral tribunal shall be in full charge of the hearings and shall conduct the oral proceedings."

15 See article 1701 of the Belgian Judicial Code: "the award is made after a deliberation in which all arbitrators must take part." "Taking part" does not require a physical gathering but a deliberation cannot be dispensed with. With regard to the requirement of a physical gathering for the deliberations, the text of article 823 of the Italian Code of Civil Procedure is noteworthy, in that it provides that "[a]ny arbitrator may request that the award, or a part thereof, be deliberated by the arbitrators meeting in person". If an arbitrator refuses to participate in the deliberations, the president (and the other arbitrator) will have to address that difficulty, all the while keeping the "defecting" arbitrator informed and giving him the opportunity to opine on every question. Informing the parties of such a situation may or may not be opportune. However, see article 1052(2) of the German Code of Civil Procedure, which requires that the parties be informed of the remaining members' intention to make an award without the arbitrator who has refused to participate in the vote. Section 20(1) of the English Arbitration Act 1996 could be read as meaning that delegation to the president is allowed for any decision, including the award: "Where the parties have agreed that there is to be a chairman, they are free to agree what the functions of the chairman are going to be in relation to the making of decisions, orders and awards." According to Merkin, "[i]t is to be presumed, however, that the chairman cannot have the power to issue the final award in all cases, as this in effect converts him into an umpire." See Robert Merkin, *Arbitration Act 1996*, 3rd ed. (London 2005) s. 20, p. 64. Whether the parties can even allow the latter form of delegation is debatable. Would it require the assent of the tribunal? Would the award rendered by the president be deemed to have been handed down by a three-member tribunal or by a sole arbitrator? This could result in difficulties, for instance, if there were to be an application for correction of that award or

a request for its revision that is admissible and ready to be submitted to the arbitral tribunal. For a specific case, see article 1051(1) of the Dutch Code of Civil Procedure on so-called summary arbitral proceedings, providing that "the parties may agree to empower the arbitral tribunal or its chairman to render an award in summary proceedings..." (emphasis added). For a recent decision on the principle of the collegiality of deliberations, see the judgment by the French Cour de cassation, 1ère Chambre civile, 29 June 2011, *Société Papillon group corporation v. République arabe de Syrie et al.*, Rev. Arb. (2011)p. 959, with comments by Vincent Chantebout.

16   Article 1479 of the French Code of Civil Procedure expressly provides for the confidentiality of the deliberations, as do, for instance, the Swiss Rules (in article 43(2)) and the ICSID Rules (in rule 15(1)). The fundamental principle of the secrecy of deliberations is reflected, for instance, in article 9 of the IBA Rules of Ethics for International Arbitrators, which states that "the deliberations of the arbitral tribunal, and the contents of the award itself, remain confidential in perpetuity unless the parties release the arbitrators from this obligation". On the importance of maintaining the confidentiality of deliberations, see Yves Derains, 'La pratique du délibéré arbitral', in G. Aksen et al., eds., *Liber Amicorum in honour of Robert Briner* (Paris 2005) pp. 221-233 at pp. 225-226.

17   The LCIA Rules clearly make this distinction, namely in article 14(3) for procedural orders ("... the chairman may, with the prior consent of the other two arbitrators, make procedural rulings alone") and in article 26(3) for awards ("... [f]ailing a majority decision on any issue, the chairman of the Arbitral Tribunal shall decide that issue"). Likewise, the Swiss Rules make the distinction in article 31(1) (no delegation for awards) and article 31(2) (delegation is possible "in the case of questions of procedure"), as do the UNCITRAL Rules (in article 33). Cf. section 20 of the English Arbitration Act 1996, which provides for the president's casting vote for awards, procedural orders and decisions, without distinction. There does not seem to be any statute or arbitration rule specifically allowing such delegation for decisions on provisional measures. This may, in fact, raise several difficulties, especially if an order on provisional relief is made in the form of an award.

18   Article 1701(1)-(2) of the Belgian Judicial Code provides: "1. ... The award shall be made by an absolute majority of votes, unless the parties have agreed on another majority. 2. The parties may also agree that, when a majority cannot be obtained, the president or the arbitral tribunal shall have a casting vote." Article 1701(3) then goes on to set out, in some detail, the modalities for voting within the tribunal when the awarding of a sum of money is at issue and a majority cannot be obtained for any particular sum. Among the arbitration laws allowing for awards to be made by the president alone when there is no majority within the tribunal, see, for instance, section 20(3)-(4) of the English Arbitration Act 1996, article 30 of the Swedish Arbitration Act, article 189(2) of the Swiss PILA and article 1513 (3)-(4) of the French Code of Civil Procedure. It is noteworthy that article 1513 of the French Code of Civil Procedure applies only to international arbitration. As far as institutional rules are concerned, one could mention, for instance, article 31(1) of the ICC Rules, article 31(1) of the Swiss Rules, article 26 (3-4) of the LCIA Rules, articles R46 and R59 of the CAS Code and article 16 of the Arbitration Rules of the Arbitration Institute of the Stockholm Chamber of Commerce (SCC Rules). As for the (rarer) statutes and rules requiring (in some cases, unless the parties agree otherwise) that a majority be reached for awards or even for all decisions of the tribunal, see, for instance, article 29 of the UNCITRAL Model Law on International Commercial Arbitration, article 1052(1) of the German Code of Civil Procedure and article 823 of the Italian Code of

Civil Procedure, as well as rule 16(1) of the ICSID Rules and article 33(1) of the UNCITRAL Rules.

19   As perceptively observed by Claude Reymond, *supra* note 2, at p. 473, the simple fact that under many sets of rules (including the ICC Rules) the president is empowered to decide alone if need be is usually sufficient to produce a unanimous or at least a majority opinion.

20   Briner, *supra* note 2, at p. 52.

21   The delegation is certainly permitted if the parties agree or at least do not object to it. See Paris Court of Appeal, *Société Aranella c. Société Italo-Ecuadoriana*, 26 April 1985, Rev. Arb. (1985) p. 311. That being said, an absolute limit on the possibility to delegate is the need for a deliberation of any award *stricto sensu*. In view of this, when a decision is at stake, the arbitrators should be prudent in exercising their discretion to delegate powers to the president and always consider whether the decision in question should be substantively characterized as an award. Whatever the arbitrators may call it, the courts should re-qualify as an award any decision wrongly labelled as a procedural order and then quash it for violation of the mandatory requirement for deliberation if the president has adopted it by himself.

22   It is true that the ICC Commission on Arbitration's *Techniques for Controlling Time and Costs in Arbitration* (to which appendix IV of the ICC Rules refers) suggest the following in para. 26, entitled "Empowering chairman on procedural issues": "Where there is a three person tribunal, it may not be necessary for all procedural issues to be decided upon by all three arbitrators. The parties should consider empowering the chairman to decide on certain procedural issues alone. In all events, consider authorizing the chairman to sign procedural orders alone." Once again, however, this is a case of delegation by the parties.

23   See *supra* note 21.

24   Similarly, see article 1696 of the Belgian Judicial Code, article 1042(4) of the German Code of Civil Procedure and section 34(2)(f) of the English Arbitration Act 1996.

25   Jean-François Poudret and Sébastien Besson, *Comparative International Arbitration*, 2nd ed. (London, 2007) para. 642, p. 550 and the references provided in n. 514.

26   Article 816-ter of the Italian Code of Civil Procedure: "The taking of the evidence or any individual steps or activities to that end may be delegated by the arbitrators to one among them." This is also reflected in article 25(3) of the Arbitration Rules of the Chamber of Arbitration of Milan (CAM Rules). For its part, article 1039(3) of the Dutch Code of Civil Procedure provides, more specifically, that the "arbitral tribunal shall have the power to designate one of its members to examine witnesses or experts".

27   Article 1467 of the French Code of Civil Procedure reads, in relevant part, as follows: "The arbitral tribunal shall take all necessary steps concerning evidentiary and procedural matters, unless the parties authorise it to delegate such tasks to one of its members."

28   See, for instance, article 15(4) of the ICC Rules, article 14 of the Swiss Rules, article 15 of the UNCITRAL Rules, article 17(3) of the SCC Rules and article 20 of the CAM Rules, which leave the matter to the discretion of the tribunal.

29   Reymond, *supra* note 2, at p. 470. See also Born, supra note 4, at p. 1666.

30   In this sense, see article 816-ter of the Italian Code of Civil Procedure, quoted supra note 26.

31   See Ugo Draetta, *Behind the Scenes in International Arbitration* (Huntington, 2011) especially ch. IV (The Arbitrators) p. 53 et seq., in particular section III (The Chairperson of the Arbitral Tribunal) p. 61 et seq. In his seminal paper, Claude Reymond elegantly described

the prudent circumspection with which the presiding arbitrator should at first approach his colleagues, until he gets to know them better, including their views as to the role they are to play in the tribunal (see Reymond, *supra* note 2).

32   There is no absolute rule and the president, as well as the whole tribunal, must make decisions based on the circumstances. For example, if the procedural calendar calls for the exchange of post-hearing submissions, it may be appropriate to give either a long lead-time or a short one for the parties to prepare them. A long time limit will allow counsel to do better work, but the arbitrators' recollection of the case will have faded somewhat by the time the submissions are in. A short period means that there is less information in the submissions but more immediate mental readiness to study them. What is to be preferred will depend on the specifics of each case.

33   For instance, the president should be willing to accept it if both parties express shared views about the conduct of the procedure and/or the "style" of the award they require in a particular case. For example, if they would prefer a fast award at the expense of having every single issue dealt with in a detailed manner, he should be amenable to waiving his legal pride and forsake long legal exposés in the award unless they are indispensable.

34   Jacques Werner, 'Arbitral Chronicle V—David Ricardo and Adam Smith', *The Journal of World Investment & Trade 1* (2010) p. 128.

35   On this point, see also Derains, supra note 16, at pp. 231-232. The reference here is to decisions made by a majority rather than to dissenting opinions communicated to the parties. However, the same reasons will also apply when an arbitrator considers dissenting, albeit less cogently, as a proper dissenting opinion may to a certain extent weaken the award. On the dynamics of deliberations, see also Ugo Draetta, 'Les dynamiques du délibéré dans l'arbitrage: quelques réflexions personnelles', *RDAI/IBLJ* (2011) pp. 219-229.

36   In order to avoid the above-mentioned difficulties with respect to the fact that, once the president's opinion is out, it is difficult to withdraw, it may be advisable to state that the views so expressed are only preliminary and open to change upon discussion with the co-arbitrators. See, for instance, Briner, supra note 2, at p. 63.

37   Similarly Derains, *supra* note 16, at p. 230.

38   "Ideally, the drafting of different parts of the award will be assigned to different members of the tribunal. For instance, the procedural history may be assigned to one, the factual findings to another and the legal findings to the third. Some editing will subsequently be required, which may be done either by the President or by the member of the tribunal most familiar with the language in which the award is to be rendered." Briner, *supra* note 2, at pp. 63-64.

39   Cf. Briner, *supra* note 2, at p. 64; Reymond, *supra* note 2, at p. 480.

40   See *supra* note 19.

41   See article 15(5) of the ICC Rules. For a discussion of the differences between the various sets of rules with respect to the issue of truncated tribunals, see, for instance, Born, *supra* note 4, at pp. 1586-1592.

CHAPTER SEVEN

SECRETARIES TO ARBITRAL TRIBUNALS

Constantine Partasides

I have long felt that there are few aspects of the practice of international arbitration that better deserve the unwelcome moniker of "hypocrisy" than the approach to the role of the secretary to the tribunal.

For many years, I have watched people stand up at conferences and speak with great sanctimony about how the use of the secretary to the tribunal for anything more than a purely administrative role would amount to a derogation of responsibility by the arbitrator. Moreover, they would often get great rounds of applause for saying so.

Nevertheless, in real life arbitrations, I would see arbitrators—not always different arbitrators to those attending or indeed intervening in the above-mentioned conferences—who would make fuller use of secretaries to help them in the discharge of their function; sometimes officially, sometimes not.

It was for this reason that, almost exactly a decade ago (in 2002), I decided to write an article on the subject that some people remember by its shortened title "The Fourth Arbitrator".

1. THE FOURTH ARBITRATOR?

Some people may remember the title, but very few remember the punctuation that followed it—namely a question mark. My aim was not to propose but to question the role of secretaries to tribunals in international arbitration:

- Was it appropriate?
- Within what limits?
- When does responsible delegation become irresponsible derogation?

My conclusion was as follows. In the same way as clerks to justices are used to great effect in many national judicial forums, so secretaries to arbitral tribunals, with the consent of the parties, can legitimately add to the efficiency and professionalism of a process in which increasingly one or three arbitrators now face—and must stay on top of—the voluminous output of veritable armies of legal teams that produce great heat, sometimes light, and inevitably much paper in modern arbitration practice.

The two reasons why some said that this judicial parallel should not be extended to arbitration seemed to me not to hold water. For the sake of argument, it is worth recalling what they were.

The first reason can be stated as follows. Arbitrators, unlike judges, are selected by the parties. The selection of arbitrators, unlike judges, is *intuiti personae*. Therefore, so the theory goes, there should be no delegation by arbitrators. However, it seems to me that this theory is surely flawed. Just because judges are not personally selected does not make their delegation of the decision-making function acceptable. Whether personally selected or not, the key is to ensure that the clerk or the secretary is used appropriately to assist—rather than replace—the decision-maker. The question for both is the same: what is the appropriate level of delegation? I see no compelling reason why that question should be answered differently for arbitrators.

The second reason, which relates to the first, can be summarized as follows. Unlike arbitrators, judges cannot say "no" to a new case that comes before their court. Unlike judges, arbitrators control their docket. For this reason, so the logic goes, arbitrators are not in the same position to justify the need for the help of a young lawyer. Arbitrators, can—and should—say no if they are not in a position to accept a voluntary appointment. Once again, such logic seems to me to miss the point. If the legitimate and proper use of secretaries can assist the efficiency of the process, why deprive an arbitrator of such a facility simply because he has consented to participate in the process.

However, my faith in the institution of secretaries was not unlimited. Searching for an appropriate dividing line between the appropriate and the inappropriate, I focused on the exercise of the drafting of the award. I concluded then that arbitrators should restrict the secretary's role in drafting actual decisions, as writing is the "ultimate safeguard of intellectual control".

2. OVER THE LAST 10 YEARS

Those were my views then, and over the last ten years the role of the secretary and my views on the issue have evolved.

The institution of secretaryships is stepping out of the shadows and into the light. It is also my impression that the phenomenon of the "secret secretary" is diminishing.

There is now far more open use and acceptance of secretaries. The best proof of this is the increasing, express accommodation of the use of secretaries in the main institutional rules in the field of arbitration, such as the new UNCITRAL Arbitration Rules.

The new UNCITRAL Arbitration Rules of 2010 now explicitly accommodate the provision of assistance to the arbitral tribunal. As the *travaux préparatoires* confirm, these rules where intended to apply to secretaries to tribunals.

Thus, article 5 of the new rules, entitled "Representation and Assistance", talks of "each party" having the facility to be represented "or assisted" by persons chosen by it. It is understood and accepted that, in this context, the reference to assistance is intended to accommodate the "assistance" of a secretary for the arbitral tribunal.

In the same way, article 16, entitled "Exclusion of Liability", extends not only to arbitrators and appointing authorities but also to "any person appointed by the Arbitral Tribunal", which again is intended to accommodate arbitral secretaries.

Finally, in the same way, article 40, entitled "Definition of Cost", explicitly includes within this definition the "reasonable costs of expert advice and of other assistance required by the Arbitral Tribunal".

This express contemplation of the appointment of secretaries is to be welcomed, but it is only the first step in addressing the legitimacy gap that focuses on the role and the cost of an arbitral secretary.

3. THE LEGITIMACY GAP REMAINS

What the revision of the UNCITRAL Rules does not do is address the key question of the appropriate role and cost of arbitral secretaries. In so far as UNCITRAL is concerned, we are left with the UNCITRAL Notes on Organizing Arbitral Proceedings, which state the problem but do not provide an answer. Paragraph 27 of the notes states that:

> *"Differences in views, however, may arise if the tasks include legal research and other professional assistance to the arbitral tribunal (e.g. collecting case law or published commentaries on legal issues defined by the arbitral tribunal, preparing summaries from case law and publications, and sometimes also preparing drafts of procedural decisions or drafts of certain parts of the award, in particular those concerning the facts of the case). Views or expectations may differ especially where a task of the secretary is similar to professional functions of the arbitrators. Such a role of the secretary is in the view of some commentators inappropriate or is appropriate only under certain conditions, such as that the parties agree thereto. However, it is typically recognized that it is important to ensure that the secretary does not perform any decision-making function of the arbitral tribunal."*

Those same questions are yet to be answered by other institutional guidance. This brings us to the ICC's Note on the Appointment of Administrative Secretaries by Arbitral Tribunals of 1995, which provides that:

1. arbitral tribunals themselves must verify that the prospective secretary "satisfies requirements of independence";
2. the secretary's duties are to be "limited" to administrative tasks, and the secretary will avoid becoming "involved" in decision-making, or expressing "opinions" in respect of the issues in dispute; and

3. the Costs are to be "normally" satisified from the tribunal's fees awarded by the court, soas to ensure that costs are not increased.

The Bureau of the ICC Court (its policy unit) is currently in the process of considering an update of this Note. As the work of the Bureau continues, it is my hope that the institutional position does not remain out of step with present practice and reality.

In particular, it is my hope to see an increasing recognition of the fact that many responsible arbitrators habitually delegate activities that go beyond the purely administrative to diligent secretaries without it impacting inappropriately on the full and proper discharge by the arbitrators of their decision-making function.

A refusal to recognize such present practice will compel arbitrators to continue to be less than transparent about the current reality, and so the double-speak—or hypocrisy—will continue in a way that can only be damaging to the legitimacy of the arbitral process.

Simply stated, it is my view that the new ICC Note must address this *décalage* and that it must do so in a way that is consistent with the present practice.

Let me take this opportunity to add my own contribution to this process by making two observations. The first concerns the appropriate scope of a secretary's duties, and the second concerns the important question of the allocation of the costs of using a secretary.

4. SCOPE OF SECRETARY'S DUTIES

As to the appropriate role to be played by a secretary, I would suggest that there need be nothing inappropriate in an arbitrator making use of the services of a young lawyer to become better informed as to the substance of the case by helping him or her to digest the arguments and the evidence presented by the parties during the course of the proceedings. I would further suggest that there is no reason why a secretary cannot assist an arbitrator in preparing first drafts of procedural orders arrived at by the arbitral tribunal. Indeed, in the same way, I would suggest that there exists no good reason why a secretary cannot, under careful supervision, legitimately assist an arbitrator with the production of a first draft of those parts of the award that are uncontroversial (e.g., the description of the procedural history or factual background of the dispute).

Beyond this, it is for the individual arbitrator to decide whether he or she can delegate the full drafting of the award to a secretary without jeopardizing decision-making control. On this sensitive subject, dogmatism is unhelpful. For some people, the act of drafting is the ultimate safeguard of intellectual control. For others, the same level of control can be achieved without producing the first draft.

Ultimately, this must be a question for the arbitrator's judgment. If the arbitrator gets such a significant decision wrong, then the problem is not with the institution of secretaryship but with the choice of arbitrator.

5. ALLOCATION OF COST

On the important question of cost, my observation follows the same logic as above. Used properly, a secretary can assist in ensuring the quality and the efficiency of the arbitral process. If the parties are persuaded of this, then there should be no reason in principle why the parties should not pay for such a service.

However, such a general principle must be accompanied by some important constraints. First, the use of secretaries should be an efficiency, rather than lead to a duplication of costs, for the parties. Thus, for example, there is a case for not charging all of the time spent by a secretary attending an oral hearing where that time is largely if not entirely duplicated by the arbitrator's own time. Second, certain limits should be imposed on the amounts charged for a secretary's time. In order to ensure that a secretary does not usurp the role of the arbitrator, there may be a case for setting a cap on the hourly rate of secretaries that would effectively disqualify lawyers of a certain seniority from serving as secretaries.

I conclude by acknowledging that these ideas are obviously incomplete and could undoubtedly be developed. For now, their aim is simply to encourage the beginning of a process that will hopefully end with the use of secretaries being recognized and regulated in a way that accords with—rather than denies—our present reality.

CHAPTER EIGHT

IMMUNITY AND LIABILITY OF ARBITRATORS: WHAT IS THE PROPER BALANCE?

Eduardo Silva Romero

There is to our knowledge no sociological data—specific cases on the liability of international arbitrators—permitting us to assert that the topic addressed in this article is relevant. There are various reasons for this.

First, it is in our view evident that international arbitrators must—and very much do—care about their reputation and prestige. To put it bluntly, should an international arbitrator be sued successfully by one of the parties to a dispute, it is very likely that this arbitrator would be excluded from the international arbitration business.

Second, our research has revealed that the only cases concerning the liability of arbitrators have been domestic. However, we have found no precedent indicating that the rules set out in these cases could somehow be applied in international settings. However, to the extent that the issue of an arbitrator's liability is governed by basic rules of contract law (*droit des obligations*),[1] one can explore and elaborate on the different potential legal grounds that could be relied upon by parties to an arbitration that would like to sue an arbitrator.

At this point, the following questions arise. Do we want to draw a legal map for losing parties that are looking to sue the arbitrator who rendered a decision adverse to their interests? Are we not under a duty to refuse to write papers that could endanger the integrity and fate of international arbitration? In our view, we should therefore only address the topic of liability of international arbitrators in order to send a strong message of caution to losing parties that, put simply, international arbitrators should only be liable in very exceptional, extraordinary circumstances.

The above propositions are not motivated by a sectarian, partisan defence of the international arbitrators' community. Rather, they flow from the principle that all adjudicators need to have sufficient calm to adjudicate disputes that have been entrusted to them. Accordingly, the guiding proposition of these observations is this: the integrity of international arbitration must be preserved by limiting as far as possible party claims against arbitrators based on adverse awards.

Lack of calm when trying to resolve a dispute may affect an international arbitrator's impartiality. No adjudicator should examine a case with the feeling—let alone under the threat—that one of the parties could eventually sue. This is the reason why, in various legal systems, references have been made to a so-called "immunity of arbitrators".[2] The rationale behind such an immunity is that all those fulfilling a jurisdictional mission, including those private persons called "arbitrators", should be protected by immunity in order that they may resolve a dispute calmly and, hence, impartially.[3]

However, the word "immunity" is ambiguous. It seems that, at the first stage in the evolution of this issue, "immunity" implied a lack of responsibility. In other words, the arbitrator would never be liable to the parties. This is still what Article 21 of the Washington Convention provides today.[4] It was traditionally also the position of US and UK law (in the latter case prior to the Arbitration Act 1996).[5] From a totally opposite perspective, the word "immunity" was referred to in some old French decisions as grounds for holding that arbitrators should have little or no immunity.[6]

The positions described above reflect two different philosophical conceptions of the mission of the arbitrator. Those defending the idea of "immunity" consider that an arbitrator is a judge.[7] This is the conception that still exists in many Latin American countries. Conversely, those arguing against providing any immunity in favour of arbitrators regard them as simple contractors.[8] However, this old clash between different conceptions of the arbitrator's mission is irrelevant today when defining whether and to what extent an arbitrator could be liable to the parties.

Indeed, there seems to be a general consensus today that there is no absolute immunity in favour of arbitrators and that arbitrators should be liable to the parties for fraud (*fraude*) and intentional wrongdoing (*dol*). This consensus is expressed in two ways. First, from a negative perspective, Section 29 of the UK Arbitration Act 1996[9] states that arbitrators enjoy immunity unless their bad faith is established. Second, from an affirmative perspective, Spanish law,[10] for example, provides that arbitrators are liable in some limited cases such as fraud, wilful misconduct and intentional wrongdoing.

There also seems to be consensus on the point that the mere negligence of an arbitrator is covered by immunity, meaning that arbitrators are not liable to the parties for mere negligence.

Today's academic debate only pertains to the question whether gross negligence (*faute lourde*) is covered by the arbitrator's immunity. In his treatise on international commercial arbitration, Gary Born,[11] addressing this issue *in abstracto* (or as a policy manifesto), asserts that gross negligence should be covered by immunity and that arbitrators should not be liable for gross negligence. From a theoretical standpoint, Born's opinion may be right in common law jurisdictions. In civil law jurisdictions, however, there is often a principle pursuant to which gross negligence (*faute lourde*) is legally assimilated to intentional wrongdoing (*dol*).[12]

However, we submit that the question whether gross negligence (*faute lourde*) is covered by the immunity of arbitrators cannot be solved in abstracto. In our view, a fact-driven, case-by-case, *in concreto* approach must be employed. In this context, three factual situations, among many other potential scenarios, can be illustrative.

In the first situation, an arbitrator does not comply with certain time-limits because he or she is unavailable. It is not absolutely clear to us that this situation could be characterized as gross negligence. In most cases, delays in the proceedings may be produced by different, concurrent causes. However, if the delay can be characterized as gross negligence, immunity should not be granted. A lack of availability pertains to the qualities required of the adjudicator and not to the mission of adjudication. In addition, this situation could give rise to a denial of justice that should not be condoned.

The second situation is one where the arbitrator incorrectly applies the applicable law. This could be a gross negligence situation. However, it clearly pertains to the mission of adjudication. If the parties could successfully sue an arbitrator for an incorrect application of the applicable law, arbitrators might lose the calm and impartiality needed to accomplish their mission. It therefore seems to us that such a situation should be covered by immunity. In other words, arbitrators should not be liable to parties for incorrectly applying the applicable law. A different, more problematic situation would be one in which the arbitrator, in spite of specific pleadings from all parties on a point of law, simply does not apply it at all.

The third and final situation is one where an arbitrator resigns without cause. There are two reasons for concluding that this situation—which could amount to gross negligence—should not be covered by immunity. First, the situation does not pertain to the mission of adjudication. Second, the situation could give rise to a denial of justice.

***

In conclusion, what is the proper balance between the immunity and liability of arbitrators? We submit—using a negative approach—that the general rule should provide for the immunity of arbitrators and that liability should only arise in three exceptional, extraordinary situations: (i) fraud; (ii) intentional wrongdoing; and (iii) gross negligence—especially if it results in a denial of justice, except when it pertains to the mission of adjudicating the dispute. Immunity should apply in order to guarantee the calm and impartiality needed to accomplish the jurisdictional mission, not to exempt arbitrators from fulfilling the *sine qua* non conditions of their office: independence, availability, applying the law chosen by the parties, and not resigning without cause.

Such a balance seems to have been struck in Section 29 of the UK Arbitration Act 1996. However, the concept of "bad faith" contained therein is ambiguous, and we therefore submit that the decision of the Paris Court of Appeal of 1 March 2011 in the *Azran case* strikes a better balance:[13]

> *"Whereas ... the arbitrator is invested with a mission that is both contractual and judicial in nature, which he must complete with conscientiousness, independence and impartiality; whereas, acting as a judge, he enjoys*

a jurisdictional immunity such that he is only liable for his personal misconduct which, to be sufficient to hold him liable, must amount to wilful conduct amounting to fraud, gross negligence or a denial of justice…".

The issue, in fine, will henceforth be to identify the factual situations that could (and perhaps should) be characterized as instances of "gross negligence".

Endnotes:

1   Clay Thomas, *L'arbitre* (Dalloz, 2001) pp. 705-706, para. 928.

2   E. Gaillard and J. Savage (eds.), 'Part 3: Chapter II—The Status of the Arbitrators', in *Fouchard Gaillard Goldman on International Commercial Arbitration* (Kluwer Law International, 1999) para. 1086; Gary B. Born, 'Chapter 12: Rights and Duties of International Arbitrators—B. Status of International Arbitrators', in *International Commercial Arbitration* (Kluwer Law International, 2009) pp. 1654-1657; Thomas, *supra* note 1, at pp. 456-457, para. 570.

3   Thomas, *supra* note 1, at p. 451, para. 565; Born, *supra* note , at pp. 1654-1655; Nigel Blackaby, Constantine Partasides, Alain Redfern and Martin Hunter, 'Powers, Duties, and Jurisdiction of an Arbitral Tribunal', in *Redfern and Hunter on International Arbitration* (Oxford University Press, 2009) p. 331, § 5.54.

4   Convention on the Settlement of Investment Disputes between States and Nationals of Other States (Washington Convention) (1965), Article 21: "[Arbitrators] *shall enjoy immunity from legal process with respect to acts performed by them in the exercise of their functions, except when the Centre waives this immunity.*"

5   Gaillard and Savage, *supra* note 2, at pp. 592-593, § 1086; Born, *supra* note, at pp. 1654-1655.

6   Born, *supra* note 3, at p. 1658.

7   Id., at pp. 1598 and 1600.

8   Thomas, *supra* note 1, at p. 704, para. 928; Born, *supra* note 3, at p. 1597.

9   UK Arbitration Act 1996, Section 29: "(1) An arbitrator is not liable for anything done or omitted in the discharge or purported discharge of his functions as arbitrator unless the act or omission is shown to have been in bad faith. (2) Subsection (1) applies to an employee or agent of an arbitrator as it applies to the arbitrator himself. (3) This section does not affect any liability incurred by an arbitrator by reason of his resigning (but see section 25)."

10   David J.A. Cairns and Alejandro López Ortiz, 'Spain's Consolidated Arbitration Law', in Miguel Ángel Fernández-Ballesteros and David Arias (eds), *Spain Arbitration Review / Revista del Club Español del Arbitraje* 13 (Wolters Kluwer España, 2012) pp. 49-73: Arbitration Law 60/2003 (incorporating 2009 and 2011 amendments), Article 21.1: "1. Acceptance obliges the arbitrators and, where applicable, the arbitral institution to comply faithfully with their responsibilities, being, if they do not do so, liable for the damage and losses they cause by reason of bad faith, recklessness or fraud. Where the arbitration is entrusted to an arbitral institution, the injured party shall have a direct action against the institution, regardless of any actions for compensation available against the arbitrators.

     The arbitrators or the arbitral institutions on their behalf shall take out civil liability insurance or an equivalent guarantee, to the amount established by the corresponding regulation. State entities and arbitral systems forming part of or dependent on the public administrations are exempt from taking out this insurance or equivalent guarantee."

11   Born, *supra* note , at p. 1662.

12   French Court of Cassation, Commercial Division, Judgment of 3 April 1990, No. 88-14871: "*gross negligence is characterized by an extremely serious behaviour bordering on wilful misconduct and indicating the inability of the debtor of the obligation to fulfil the contractual mission he had accepted.*" French Court of Cassation, Commercial Division, Judgment of 27 September 2011, No. 10-21362.

13   Paris Court of Appeal, *Azran v. Schirer, Leclercq, Nahum and the company SAS Consultaudit,* Judgment of 1 March 2011, No. 09/22701.

CHAPTER NINE

DO INSTITUTIONS REALLY ADD VALUE TO THE ARBITRAL PROCESS?

Karl-Heinz Böckstiegel

1. INSTITUTIONAL v. *AD HOC* ARBITRATION

I should perhaps start this article by indicating that my views are based primarily on my experience as an arbitrator and on my various functions in arbitration institutions at present and in the past.

Both in commercial and investment arbitration, the principle choice is between institutional and *ad hoc* arbitration. In fact, both of these choices are frequently found in practice.

Commercial contracts, in their arbitration clauses, mostly express a choice for just one of these two options. In practice, a large majority appears to prefer institutional arbitration. In contrast, investment contracts between states and foreign investors, as well as Bilateral Investment Treaties (BITs), often provide for a choice of several kinds of arbitration: institutional arbitration (under the rules of various arbitral institutions) or *ad hoc* arbitration (usually with a reference to the UNCITRAL Arbitration Rules).

The simple choice for ad hoc arbitration, which is sometimes found in domestic contracts, seems to be very rare in international contracts and state treaties. There are obvious reasons for this. Domestic arbitration clauses can rely on the domestic arbitration law of a particular state as a framework for the arbitral process, and the parties will mostly be ready to go along with this. On the other hand, there is no such generally accepted and applicable framework for international arbitrations. The New York Convention only deals with the recognition and enforcement of awards, and parties from different national backgrounds will most often try to avoid the unwarranted interference of the national courts at the seat of arbitration.

Therefore, if for some reason the parties cannot agree on an arbitral institution, the compromise is often to select the UNCITRAL Rules, since they provide for *ad hoc* arbitration but also offer a framework for the procedure. In particular, they provide a default procedure, in case a party does not appoint an arbitrator or an arbitrator is challenged, by authorizing an appointing authority selected by the parties or otherwise the Permanent Court of Arbitration (PCA) in The Hague to take decisions in this regard if the parties do not cooperate or cannot agree.

This shows that, unless the parties are ready to accept the default provisions of the domestic law at the seat of arbitration, which will normally authorize the domestic courts, they have to select institutional arbitration or at least the UNCITRAL Rules, including the latter's appointing authority.

2. DIFFERENT ROLES OF ARBITRAL INSTITUTIONS

But *which* institution should the parties select? Here, I will not enter into a subjective discussion about which arbitral institution is "the best", one reason being that there is no general answer.

First of all, it is possible to distinguish between institutions that are well-suited for international arbitration procedures and others that are not. Even if one ignores the many institutions that have been founded with ambitious claims but are never chosen in practice, distinctions can be made among the well-known arbitral institutions. Over many years in the field, I have gathered experience as an arbitrator in most of these institutions and, without mentioning names, there are certainly some that did not seem to be well-suited for or efficient in conducting international arbitral procedures. To some extent, this negative experience was due to the staff of those institutions not being sufficiently trained or at least not sufficiently familiar with the specifics of international arbitration, as well as to organizational deficiencies such as limited lists of arbitrators or specific rules and formalities not suited for the practical demands of international arbitral procedures.

On the other hand, international institutions such as ICC, the LCIA, the PCA and ICSID, as well as national institutions involved in international arbitration, such as the German Institution of Arbitration (DIS), the Stockholm Chamber of Commerce (SCC), the Swiss Chambers' Arbitration Institution and the Vienna International Arbitral Centre (VIAC), have in my experience over many years displayed efficiency in the cases referred to them.

Among these recommended arbitral institutions, the choice must depend on the objective criteria that are most relevant to the parties. In this context, it should be noted, first and foremost, that the rules of these institutions are rather similar, since they have all been modernized and adapted to reflect the development of international arbitral practice.

However, there remain some important differences, particularly regarding the *degree of involvement of the institution* in its own arbitral procedure.

The greatest regulatory involvement is probably found in the ICC Rules, including their latest version adopted in 2012. They provide for the involvement of the ICC Court at the beginning of the procedure (in relation to the terms of reference) and at the end of the procedure (in the scrutiny of the draft award). However, the ICC Secretariat, though informed of the progress of the procedure, will usually not get involved in the management of the case or the communications between the parties and the tribunal.

In contrast, in ICSID cases, the secretariat forms the continuous channel of communication between the parties and the tribunal. Moreover, the ICSID Convention provides for an annulment procedure after an award is issued.

Since its more recent development into a leading arbitral institution, operating mostly under the UNCITRAL Rules that grant wide discretion to the arbitral tribunal, the PCA is often chosen to assist the tribunal in the administration of particularly large and complex cases. Similarly, the LCIA and the national arbitral institutions that are also regularly chosen for international disputes probably provide the widest discretion to the parties and the tribunal in terms of case management and their ability to shape each procedure to the particularities of the case.

Of course, the different *methods and scales for the remuneration of the arbitrators* may also be considered relevant and may also have an impact depending on the particularities of the case. Here, the major distinction is between remuneration relying on the amount in dispute and remuneration based on an hourly rate. Views on this can be a matter of subjective judgment and personal background. However, it may also make a significant practical difference depending on the case, the amount in dispute and the volume of work and time required from the arbitrators.

In the context of continuing complaints about arbitration becoming too expensive, it is worth noting—as statistics show and as confirmed at the 2011 IFCAI Conference in Berlin—that in general more than 90% of arbitration costs are incurred by the parties themselves for counsel, witnesses and experts, their battles over documents and so forth. The influence of the arbitral institutions over these costs is rather limited. Any changes regarding the very small percentage going to the administrative charge of the institution and the fees of the arbitrators will therefore have a relatively small impact on the general level of arbitration costs. Moreover, even if the institution or the arbitrators could exercise some influence to reduce the parties' general arbitration costs, any effort to introduce a slimmer procedure would soon run up against the limit of the parties' understandable desire and their and their counsel's due process right to fully present their case as they consider necessary.

In view of all these criteria and options, one obviously cannot say that one of the institutions available for the efficient administration of cases is better than any other. It is up to the parties to decide which of the above-mentioned distinctions are most relevant to them with regard to a particular contract, arbitration clause or case.

3. SOME ESSENTIAL FACTORS OF INTERACTION

In this section, I will briefly consider some key factors that, based on my many years of experience with arbitral institutions, appear to be most conducive to a successful and efficient interaction between the institution, the parties and the tribunal.

a. Efficient staff at the institution

Only after experiencing on several occasions what kind of difficulties can arise if the tribunal is faced with incompetent staff did I realize how much the swift and efficient management of a procedure can be jeopardized in such situations. Obviously, the greater the involvement of the institution in the conduct of the procedure, the more this applies. However, much can also go wrong at the start or end of the procedure, for example in the management and control of arbitration costs and timely deposits. In this context, particular problems include the staff not being sufficiently qualified or at least not sufficiently familiar with the particular demands of international as opposed to domestic arbitration.

b. Flexibility of procedure within the framework of the rules

Quite often, staff who are not sufficiently familiar with the particularities of international arbitration will stick to particular routines and formalities that they have seen before and will not understand or be willing to use the discretion allowed by the rules of the institution in order to shape the procedure. One of the great advantages of arbitration over litigation is lost, namely the ability to adapt the individual procedure to deal with the specific demands of the case in the most efficient way possible.

c. Informal exchanges with the institution

While the rules of each arbitral institution obviously provide a framework for the role of the institution, the parties and the arbitrators in the conduct of the procedure, in practice it would sometimes be easier and cause fewer complications and delays if an informal prior exchange could take place regarding the interpretation of certain provisions in the rules and/or their practical application in similar earlier cases. Once again, however, such an informal interaction can only be successful if there are experienced participants on both sides of the exchange. In addition, mandatory transparency would have to be maintained so as not to give one party an advantage over the other.

d. Involving the parties beyond what is mandatory

While respecting the rules of every arbitral institution, I would suggest that both the institution and the arbitrators should make an effort to obtain prior comments from the parties before major procedural decisions are taken and issued. An example of this from the institutional side is that the ICC Court regularly informs the parties in advance that it intends to raise the deposit for arbitration costs before the decision is issued. From a tribunal's perspective, it will often be wise to send a draft of an initial procedural ruling on the further procedure or a procedural order deciding the details of an upcoming hearing to the parties (and perhaps also to the institution) asking for comments, in order to make sure that no essential element or particularity of the case is overlooked.

e. Suppressing one's ego

Finally, I wish to make a rather subjective recommendation, namely that all those involved in the interaction between the institution, the parties and the tribunal should suppress their egos as much as possible. I have often seen in disputes that communication and potential agreements were hindered, delayed or even prevented because some participants considered it a personal offence that their views were not accepted. Sometimes, arbitrators with great reputations and experience, or who hold very high positions in their field of work outside of arbitration, regard it as a lack of "respect" if other participants in the exchange take a different view from their own. Sometimes, barristers or other high-level counsel for a party seem unable to accept that the procedure proceeds in a manner to which they are not accustomed. Sometimes, representatives of arbitral institutions seem to be offended and unable to accept that a particular procedural decision does not follow "what has always been done".

My suggestion to all those involved in this type of interaction, regardless of one's level of experience, is to listen, keep an open mind and be ready for compromise if it is conducive to the smooth conduct of the procedure within the applicable rules.

4. CONCLUSION

In conclusion, my response to the question in the title of this article is as follows.

First, institutions do indeed add value to the arbitral process.

Second, for most disputes in international arbitration, the involvement of an institution or at least an appointing authority under the UNCITRAL Rules is highly recommended in order to avoid unwarranted interference by national courts.

Third, the choice of institution depends on the relative importance the parties attach to the various and varying qualities of the arbitral institutions with regard to the case at hand.

Finally, in the interaction between the institution, the parties, and the arbitrators, certain essential factors should be taken into account in order to achieve the most efficient procedure possible.

CHAPTER TEN

RECIPROCAL DUTIES OF INSTITUTIONS AND ARBITRATORS

Peter Leaver, QC

1. THE CASE FOR ADMINISTERED ARBITRATION

Much of what I will be discussing in this article will be familiar to most readers and is relevant to all arbitral institutions. I am not aware of any definitive research on the ratio of administered to *ad hoc* international commercial arbitrations. However, received wisdom would suggest that this is somewhere between 40/60 and 60/40—let us call it 50/50. In this article, I will refer on a number of occasions to the rules of the LCIA. I do so not in order to make any particular point in favour of the LCIA but rather to illustrate the similarity between the procedures of the LCIA and the ICC and other institutions. For a comparative study of the rules of many of the arbitral institutions worldwide, it is worthwhile attending the Annual Conference of the Swiss Arbitration Association, because copies of the rules of most of the arbitral institutions in the world are always available there. A comparison of the rules of the various institutions demonstrates that the vast majority of procedures are common to all institutions. The differences are, in my view, comparatively minor and insignificant.

The case for administered arbitration includes:

(i)   certainty in drafting/a proven set of terms and conditions;
(ii)   taking care of the fundamentals without recourse to state courts;
- appointment of arbitrators, including default;
- challenges;
- multi-party arbitrations;
- interim measures;
- progressing the arbitration in the absence of a party;
(iii)   managing costs and time; and
(iv)   selection and appointment of arbitrators.

2. THE DUTIES OF THE ARBITRATOR

Prior to his appointment, the arbitrator has a duty to consider the identity of the parties (including associated companies and controlling interests) and the parties' counsel, in order to be able to complete his statement of independence accurately and honestly. In addition, he must assume a continuing duty to disclose any new circumstances, between the date of his appointment and the date on which the arbitration is concluded, that might give rise to doubts as to his independence or impartiality. Such duties are set out in materially identical terms, for example, in Articles 11(2) and 11(3) of the ICC Rules, and Rules 10.4 and 10.5 of the SIAC Rules. Prior to his appointment, the arbitrator also has a duty to consider whether he can devote sufficient time to the proceedings and to decline the appointment if he cannot.[1]

Once the arbitrator has been appointed, most institutional rules provide him with a clear statement of general duties, which usually mirror the UNCITRAL Model Law and/or (as in the case of the LCIA Rules) the procedural law at the most commonly selected seat.

The basic standard is set out in Article 18 of the Model Law:

> *"The parties shall be treated with equality and each party shall be given a full opportunity of presenting his case."*

It is expanded in Article 17.1 of the UNCITRAL Arbitration Rules:

> *"... the arbitral tribunal may conduct the arbitration in such manner as it considers appropriate, provided that the parties are treated with equality and that at an appropriate stage of the proceedings each party is given a reasonable opportunity of presenting its case. The arbitral tribunal, in exercising its discretion, shall conduct the proceedings so as to avoid unnecessary delay and expense and to provide a fair and efficient process for resolving the parties' dispute."*

Article 14.1 of the LCIA Rules similarly provides that the tribunal has a general duty at all times:[2]

> *"(i) to act fairly and impartially between all parties, giving each a reasonable opportunity of putting its case and dealing with that of its opponent; and*
>
> *(ii) to adopt procedures suitable to the circumstances of the arbitration, avoiding unnecessary delay or expense, so as to provide fair and efficient means for the final resolution of the parties' dispute."*

These, then, are the overarching duties of the arbitrator. Prior to accepting appointment, he must consider whether he is free of conflicts and whether he can devote sufficient time to ensure the expeditious conduct of the arbitration. Thereafter, he must set a realistic procedural timetable (in consultation with the parties), from which he should not deviate without good cause.

Such is the importance placed by the LCIA Court on this duty that, under Article 10.2 of the LCIA Rules, an arbitrator in breach of this obligation may be considered unfit in the opinion of the LCIA Court and may be removed. Similarly, under Rule 14.3 of the SIAC Rules, the Chairman of the Centre may at his discretion remove any arbitrator "if he is not fulfilling his functions in accordance with the Rules or within the prescribed time limits."

There are a number of other specific duties to which reference must be made.

First, the arbitrator has a specific duty to ensure that the institution is kept fully informed of progress, which will generally be achieved simply by copying the institution on relevant correspondence between the tribunal and the parties.[3]

Second, under Article 24.2 of the LCIA Rules, though not under the rules of institutions charging on an *ad valorem* basis, the arbitrator must ascertain "at all times" from the secretariat that the institution is in sufficient funds to cover the ongoing costs of the arbitration, absent which he may not proceed.

For this purpose, and for the assessment of the costs of the arbitration for inclusion in his award, the arbitrator must keep a careful and accurate record of time spent.

A great deal naturally turns on the outcome of any arbitration, whether that outcome is purely monetary or the consequence of some declaratory relief. In some cases, the outcome has a direct impact on the survival of businesses.

One of the most common charges currently laid at the door of arbitration is the failure of tribunals to issue their awards in timely fashion. The tribunal must, therefore, strive to deliver its award within a reasonable time of the conclusion of the proceedings. For example, the ICC Rules and the Rules of the Camera Arbitrale Milano both set a presumptive deadline for the final award of six months from the finalization of the Terms of Reference and/or constitution of the tribunal, while the SIAC Rules go even further. In particular, Rule 28.2 of the SIAC Rules requires the tribunal to submit a draft award to the Registrar of the Centre for approval within 45 days of the date on which the tribunal declared the proceedings closed, unless the parties agree otherwise. In the event of unavoidable delays, the parties should be kept apprised and not be left in the dark.

3. THE DUTIES OF THE INSTITUTION

If the arbitrator's overarching duty is to decide the dispute in a fair, timely and cost-effective manner, the reciprocal overarching duty of the institutions is to provide efficient and cost-effective administrative services to support the arbitrator and the parties in the achievement of this end.

It is often said that the single most important responsibility of an institution (after satisfying itself that there is *prima facie* jurisdiction) is to get the right tribunal in place as quickly as possible.

This will always mean proceeding expeditiously with the constitution of the tribunal, in accordance with the contractual timetable and/or the timetable set out in the institution's rules. Thus, for example, Article 13(2) of the Rules of the Arbitration Institute of the Stockholm Chamber of Commerce provides that, where the tribunal is to consist of a single arbitrator, the parties have ten days to jointly appoint the arbitrator, failing which the Board itself will appoint the arbitrator. Similar provisions can be found in Article 12(3) of the ICC Rules and Article 14.5 of the SIAC Rules. It may also mean expediting the appointment of the tribunal in cases of exceptional urgency (see, e.g., Article 9 of the LCIA Rules) or the appointment of an "emergency arbitrator" (see, e.g., Article 29 of the ICC Rules and Rule 5.2 of the SIAC Rules).

The first duty of the institution is thus to facilitate the selection and appointment of the arbitrator or arbitrators, whether nominated by the parties, the party nominees or the institution itself.[4]

It is, perhaps, also worth bearing in mind that the parties and the institution may have different objectives when selecting arbitrators.

Parties ultimately want to succeed in their case and may reasonably be expected to seek arbitrators whose track record and/or public statements (oral or written) suggest that they may be sympathetic to their position. Points to note in this regard include arbitrator interviews, beauty parades and so forth.

The institution, on the other hand, ultimately wants the arbitration to succeed, irrespective of the outcome. In other words, its aim it to reach a just and binding conclusion as expeditiously and cost-effectively as due process will allow.

With this in mind, the institution must provide the selected arbitrator, prior to his appointment, with sufficient information about the parties and sufficient background to the dispute to enable the arbitrator to properly consider: (a) the existence of disqualifying conflicts or the likelihood of that such conflicts will arise; (b) whether he has the requisite experience and expertise; and (c) whether he has the time to devote to the case given, for example, any early indications as to urgency and complexity.

While it is not for the institution to interfere with the proceedings or to second-guess the tribunal, it is a proper part of the institution's supporting role to monitor the timetable, as agreed or directed, and to enquire of the tribunal if it is apparent that there is slippage in the timetable for reasons of which it is unaware. The pace of an arbitration can be significantly slowed by the failure of one or both parties to cooperate, and an institution may be able to communicate with and influence an uncooperative party or a tardy tribunal.[5]

Just as the arbitrator must keep the institution fully informed, so the secretariat must pass on any correspondence that comes to it without a copy to the tribunal and remind the parties of their obligation to keep the tribunal in the loop.

Moreover, just as the arbitrator must be free of conflicts at the time of his appointment and throughout the proceedings, so the institution must be ready to deal swiftly, effectively and in an even-handed manner with any challenge that may be brought against an arbitrator. In the ICC Rules, for example, the relevant procedure is set out at Article 14. This is also a particularly significant duty in the case of the LCIA, which, uniquely, provides reasoned decisions on challenges. An institution may also provide a list of suitably qualified arbitrators to assist a party in selecting a replacement.

For the purposes of funding, the secretariat must keep the tribunal advised of the receipt and disbursement of parties' funds, and not simply leave it to the tribunal to check that there are sufficient monies to proceed.

The secretariat should therefore regularly call for interim fee notes and should apprise the tribunal of accruing administrative charges, of which tribunals sometimes do not take proper account. Thus, under Rule 30.4 of the SIAC Rules, responsibility falls on the Registrar of the Centre to direct the parties to make further advances towards the costs of the arbitration. Similarly, under Article 36 of the ICC Rules, the Secretary General is empowered to call on the parties for an advance on the costs of the arbitration, and the amount of such advance may be subject to readjustment at any time during the arbitration (under Article 36(5)).

Under Article 33 of the ICC Rules, the ICC Court scrutinizes and approves the award before it can be issued. The same is true under Rule 28.2 of the SIAC Rules, which provides that the Registrar's review is not limited to identifying clerical errors but extends even to drawing the attention of the tribunal to "points of substance". Under the LCIA Rules, it is the LCIA Court (through the Registrar) that physically issues awards to the parties. Therefore, just as there is an onus on the tribunal to render its award promptly, so there is an onus on the institution to carry out its obligations in connection with the issuing of the award; confirm the costs of the arbitration for inclusion in a final award; efficiently and expeditiously scrutinize the award (if this is the practice of the institution); and efficiently and expeditiously prepare certified copies, bind and stamp the award and dispatch it to the parties.

4. SECRETARIES TO THE TRIBUNAL

Although some aspects of this topic have already been covered, it is worth emphasizing that a line should be drawn between the services of the institution, the duties of the tribunal and the duties of secretaries to tribunals.

The duties of the secretary should neither conflict with nor duplicate those for which the parties are paying the institution nor should they constitute any delegation of the tribunal's authority.

While the institution should be willing to liaise with the secretary on administrative matters, the institution should take responsibility for such things as finalizing arrangements for hearing venues, transcripts and so forth; providing any reminders that may be required in connection with the procedural timetable; and dealing with all matters required of it under the institution's rules.

Secretaries should therefore be primarily concerned with such matters as organizing papers for the tribunal, highlighting relevant legal authorities, maintaining factual chronologies, keeping the tribunal's time sheets and so forth.

5. THE ARBITRATOR, THE INSTITUTION AND THE PARTIES

There is a further important but often overlooked catch-all provision in the ICC Rules (Article 41), the LCIA Rules (Article 32.2) and the SIAC Rules (Rule 36.2), which, if not express, should be implicit in all institutional rules. In the words of the LCIA Rules, it provides:

> *"In all matters not expressly provided for in these Rules, the LCIA Court, the Arbitral Tribunal and the parties shall act in the spirit of these Rules and shall make every reasonable effort to ensure that an award is legally enforceable."*

6. THE RESULT OF EFFECTIVE COLLABORATION

If the tribunal and the institution perform their reciprocal duties in a positive and cooperative fashion, there is every chance that the goal of every arbitration, whether institutional or *ad hoc*, will be met. That goal is the rendering of a well-drafted, reasoned and just award, on time and within budget.

In this context, I would like to mention some recent research carried out by the LCIA. An analysis of 55 recent LCIA cases that ran their course from the initial request for arbitration to the issuing of a final award suggests that such collaboration between tribunal and institution can indeed deliver on time and cost.

The LCIA's research shows that around 50% of cases administered by the LCIA were concluded within 12 months or less, and around 75% within 18 months or less.

Finally, if it is not already clear (as I hope that it is), I cannot stress sufficiently that the aim of every institution must be to add value to the proceedings in everything that it does. And, for the avoidance of doubt, every arbitrator should also share that aim.

Endnotes:

1   The LCIA India Rules provide expressly, at Article 5.3(b) that an arbitrator must, prior to appointment, confirm his ability to devote sufficient time, and, of course, the ICC's statement of independence now includes a detailed "*availability*" section.

2   The parallel provisions in the ICC rules are at Article 22 and 11(5), under which arbitrators "undertake to carry out their responsibilities in accordance with the Rules". There are similar provisions in the SIAC rules at Rule 16.

3   See, for example, Article 13 of the LCIA Rules. In the ICC Rules, see Article 23(2), which provides that the tribunal must send the Court the agreed Terms of Reference, and Article 24(2), which provides: "The procedural timetable and modifications thereto shall be communicated to the Court."

4   In 2010, 41% of the arbitrators appointed by the LCIA Court were selected by the parties; 10% by the party nominees; and 49% by the LCIA Court itself.

5   As noted in *Russell on Arbitration* (23rd ed.) at 3-053.

CHAPTER ELEVEN

TRANSPARENCY: IS IT REALLY NEEDED AND TO WHAT EXTENT?

Judith Gill, QC

1. INTRODUCTION

This topic brings to mind a visit some years ago to Antonio Parra, then Deputy Secretary-General at ICSID, in Washington. There was some consternation within ICSID at that time, due to criticism in the American media of the way in which arbitration tribunals under NAFTA were operating.

It started with a 2002 piece on a talk show on the US Public Broadcasting Service (PBS) by Bill Moyers called "Trading Democracy".[1] The report focused on NAFTA and the use of Chapter 11, described as "an obscure section", which it was alleged was being used by foreign multinational corporations to "attack public laws that protect our health—and our environment—even to attack the American judicial system". This was described as being "like a sophisticated extortion racket" in which "secret NAFTA tribunals can force taxpayers to pay billions of dollars in lawsuits filed by [foreign] corporations against the United States", with "claims being decided not in open court but in what has become a system of private justice, in secret tribunals".

The PBS piece was prompted by the well-known *Methanex and Loewen* cases.[2] Of course, these were not the first claims under Chapter 11 of NAFTA. Their distinguishing feature, however, was that they were brought against the United States, which, in the journalist's view, made them an affront to the American judicial system.

This broadcast was followed a few months later in April 2002 by a Business Week article entitled "The Highest Court You've Never Heard Of".[3] Again discussing *Loewen*, the piece described how the Canadian investor went to "an obscure three-judge panel" whose decision cannot be appealed. It suggested that, due to some NAFTA "fine print" (a reference to Chapter 11), this case and others were going through a "little-known and highly secretive process".

It is easy to understand why ICSID would be concerned at this media outcry over private arbitration tribunals holding hearings behind closed doors and rendering awards deciding disputes worth millions of dollars, on matters of public interest such as health and the environment, between private investors and state parties. Resolving such disputes is, after all, one of the central purposes of ICSID as an institution.[4]

The concerns expressed in these media pieces about the lack of transparency have been addressed to some extent by ICSID. Its Arbitration Rules were amended in 2006 in order to provide some scope for amicus briefs and public hearings,[5] thereby meeting to some extent at least the demands for greater openness in proceedings and participation by interested third parties representing the public. Some hearings are now held in public and can be accessed on the Internet.[6] Moreover, the fact that ICSID awards are so often made public (and even those that are not formally accessible through ICSID online are often circulated widely among practitioners in the field) means that at least it cannot be said that the decisions reached and the reasoning of the tribunals involved are kept secret.[7]

Of course, investment arbitration such as that conducted under the auspices of ICSID might be said to warrant greater transparency, given that investors seeking to hold host states or state entities to account potentially raises issues of concern to a broader audience than simply the parties to the dispute. These cases often involve compliance by the state with its public international law obligations and may impact on its exercise of sovereign powers such as the ability to regulate. Moreover, any resulting award made against a state or state entity is likely to impose demands on the public purse.

Is it right, though, to regard this shift towards greater transparency in investment arbitration as being simply driven by its particular characteristics? Or do at least some of the concerns raised apply equally to commercial arbitration? While it may be easy to detect the public interest involved in a private tribunal ordering a government to pay hundreds of millions of dollars in compensation from taxpayers' monies, the same applies to state-owned enterprises and corporate entities in which the public retain a substantial interest through government subsidies, because ultimately it is the public that will likely foot the bill. Even if confined to state parties, why should the transparency deemed appropriate in an ICSID case not apply equally to those conducted under other institutional or *ad hoc* rules?

This issue has been toyed with,[8] but the fact remains that the greater openness in proceedings and participation of third parties introduced by ICSID has not been adopted more broadly by other institutions, even in investment arbitration cases involving states. Rather, arbitration involving state parties conducted under other institutional rules or the *ad hoc* UNCITRAL Rules usually remains confidential unless both parties agree on disclosure, even where matters of public interest are at stake.[9]

The traditional response to criticism of this state of affairs is a staunch defence of the right of parties to choose to have their dispute heard in private and to keep the result to themselves, whether or not they are state parties. Indeed confidentiality is traditionally considered a defining characteristic of arbitration in many jurisdictions. Since the Australian ruling in *Esso v. Plowden*,[10] it has been clear that it would be wrong to assume that approach is universal, yet it is not obvious why an arbitration conducted in London should be confidential whereas one conducted in Sydney need not be. Moreover, given the jurisdictional constraints upon ICSID arbitration, it can be no answer to suggest that the possibility of choosing the more transparent regime suffices to address any concerns.

There are a number of reasons why making awards publicly available is said to have merit, including the discipline that it imposes on the decision makers, the contribution that tribunals' decisions can make to the development of the law (particularly in those areas of the law where the referral of disputes to arbitration has become so commonplace as to effectively stymie its development through the courts) and, of course, the same policy concerns regarding transparency of the justice system that led to national courts being opened up to the public: justice must not just be done, but must be seen to be done.

The question therefore arises whether arbitration rules and institutions ought to take a more transparent approach, for example to reverse what may be the presumption of confidentiality, so that it applies only when the parties, or perhaps just one of them, affirmatively seeks it. It is noteworthy in this regard that, while the publication of awards is far from automatic or systematic, the reality is that awards regularly do appear in the form of sanitized case reports and that organizations like ICC play a role in that process. It is also far from unusual for the result of so-called confidential arbitrations to be discussed in trade and industry publications. Moreover, whether or not it is a breach of a party's confidentiality obligations, either as a matter of the curial law of the arbitration or the institutional rules applicable, the remedies available for disclosure of an award are largely ineffective: the damage is done on publication, and proof of monetary loss as a result of publication is usually extremely difficult. That is perhaps why, in some cases, one sees disclosure with no effective sanction, however much the other party objects.

Insofar as awards are concerned, it is perhaps legitimate to ask whether awards should be kept secret even in purely commercial cases or whether institutions should make them available, making it clear in their procedural rules that this will be the case absent affirmative objection by the parties.

Whether or nor arbitration awards are to be kept secret, can it ever be defensible for arbitration to be conducted without procedural transparency? That is perhaps where the role of the institutions comes most sharply into focus. They are often called upon to perform a number of key functions in the arbitration process, yet precisely how they operate and on what basis is not always clear.

There are many situations where demands for transparency in the context of arbitration institutions arise, but this article will focus on three in particular, namely the selection of arbitrators, the determination of challenges to arbitrators and the scrutiny of and amendments proposed to draft awards.

2. THE SELECTION OF ARBITRATORS

It has often been said that the selection of the tribunal is probably the most important aspect of the arbitration procedure. It frequently falls to the nominated institution to make the appointment, particularly if a party fails to make an appointment, yet how this is done is not always clear. For many institutions, there seems to be a private list—real or notional—of those who are considered suitable for selection, but exactly who is on the "list" may not be publicly disclosed.

The lists of arbitrators of some institutions are of course made public, but then there may be lists within the list. In particular, there may be a broad list of approved arbitrators that parties can see, but the list of those whom the institution would actually appoint may be rather shorter. Even an institution like ICC, which seeks input from national committees, cannot be said to be entirely transparent about who gets nominated by the national committees and why. Ultimately decisions on appointments are made by the ICC Court, but the rules expressly provide that the reasons for the decision shall not be communicated.[11]

So complete transparency is clearly missing, but does it matter? To begin with, it must be borne in mind that a decision about who to appoint as arbitrator is not a scientific matter. It involves a judgment as to who would be suitable in all the circumstances, including the subject matter of the dispute, the nationalities of the parties, the previously selected arbitrators, the geographical location of those involved, the seat of the arbitration and so on. Given the potential reputational consequences for an institution of its appointments, there is some sense in allowing the institution to be free to exercise its judgment as it deems appropriate.

Furthermore, in many cases where an arbitrator is appointed by the institution, the parties are less concerned with getting a particular individual than with having someone else make the decision on their behalf, either because they trust the institution to make a more informed choice or because it insulates them to some degree from criticism if it turns out to be a poor choice. In other words, the parties primarily want a third party to choose for them, and opening up the process would arguably lead to more challenges to the way in which that process operates.

Another factor is that, in practice, parties can, if they wish, have some input in the process. Most institutions will allow parties to make representations as to the characteristics they would wish the institution to take into account when making the appointment, such as legal background, nationality, language capability and so on.

In short, while there could undoubtedly be greater transparency in the appointment process, there are cogent reasons for maintaining the current rather more opaque practice. The system does not appear to be broken, and any attempt to fix it may itself cause problems, such as introducing a greater propensity for challenges. Ultimately, if parties are concerned about the approach an institution will take, they usually have the right to make the selection themselves or will at least have an opportunity to do so by agreement.

3. DETERMINATION OF CHALLENGES TO ARBITRATORS

The second area where issues of transparency arise concerns challenges to arbitrators. The practice of different institutions varies considerably in this regard.

Many, including ICC, do not provide reasons for its rulings on challenges to arbitrators.[12] On one level, this approach is entirely understandable, in that it is a safer course for the institution to insulate itself from claims that its decisions are inconsistent or wrongly reasoned or motivated. Moreover, it may not be practical to reduce the decision to a concise, consistent record of the applicable reasoning where it is made by a body with a substantial membership contributing to the discussion. That being said, it is often far from satisfying for a party that has unsuccessfully maintained or resisted a challenge to be told the result but not the way in which it was reached.

However, the LCIA does now make available information regarding how it deals with challenges to arbitrators. In fact, it recently published the sanitized details of challenges it has dealt with in *Arbitration International*. This is a project that was many years in the making, and time will tell the extent to which it proves useful in the context of other cases. However, it does seem to be a move in the right direction in terms of giving guidance to arbitrators and parties about the kinds of issues that may be considered to give rise to a successful challenge.

Challenges to arbitrators are necessarily fact-specific, but it is nevertheless possible and may be extremely useful to understand the parameters of acceptability by reference to other decisions of the same or different institutions. Of relevance here is the widespread acceptance of the IBA's Guidelines on Conflicts of Interest,[13] which, although not directly applicable to the way in which institutions determine challenges, have brought some clarity to the issue. These guidelines do not set a rigid standard, but the extent to which they are consulted by arbitrators, counsel and parties, as well as institutions, means that they influence decisions of the various stakeholders in this area.[14]

4. SCRUTINY OF AND AMENDMENTS PROPOSED TO DRAFT AWARDS

Finally, the question arises to what extent the institution's role regarding the scrutiny of and proposal of amendments to awards should be transparent. Once again, such transparency might be thought to unnecessarily expose the inner workings of the machine. The award in its final form will be seen by the parties. At that stage, the arbitrator will have accepted or rejected the suggestions of the institution. Why should the parties have a right to see those suggestions that the arbitrator rejected? And what is to be gained from their seeing those that he accepted? Once adopted, they form part of the award, and it does not matter whether they were suggested by the institution any more than it matters that the award is affected by many other influences on how the arbitrator approaches his task.

There may be something to be said for transparency with regard to this issue being a safety net to ensure that institutions confine their comments to form rather than inappropriately seeking to influence the substantive decision. Arguably, however, that comes back to the arbitrator in question. Arbitrators know that it is for them to make the substantive decision and that they are entitled to reject any attempt to influence that decision by the institution. Arbitrators who fail to live up to expectations in this regard may well have broader issues regarding their suitability for the role!

5. CONCLUSION

It must be right to question from time to time whether there is a need for greater transparency in arbitration, particularly as regards the role of institutions. The sort of press comments referred to at the beginning of this article may be rare, but they serve as a reminder that what seems clear and obvious to those involved in the system may be less so to others.

There is perhaps still a debate to be had about whether and, if so, how commercial awards should be published: whether the current practice of publishing sanitized awards is sufficient; whether public interest issues should influence the extent to which awards are made publicly available; and even the extent to which the parties should be assumed to want the award to be confidential.

As for the level of transparency within arbitral institutions regarding their role in the arbitration, there is undoubtedly more that could be done, especially regarding disclosure of the reasoning behind arbitrator challenges. Care is nevertheless needed, as any attempt to increase transparency may well have unforeseen and unwelcome consequences. Losing parties often look for ways to challenge an award. Shining a brighter light on the workings of institutions may provide them with further grounds for doing so, and it is hard to see that as progress.

Endnotes:

1   Transcript available at: <http://www.pbs.org/now/transcript/transcript_tdfull.html>.

2   *Methanex Corporation v. United States of America,* UNCITRAL, Final Award of the Tribunal on Jurisdiction and Merits, 3 August 2005; *The Loewen Group, Inc. and Raymond L. Loewen v. United States of America,* ICSID Case No. ARB(AF)/98/3, Award, 26 June 2003.

3   Available at: <http://www.businessweek.com/magazine/content/02_13/b3776102.htm>.

4   The International Centre for the Settlement of Investment Disputes (ICSID) was established by the 1965 Convention on the Settlement of Investment Disputes between States and Nationals of Other States, also known as the Washington Convention. As the name suggests, its primary purpose is to facilitate the settlement of investment disputes between states and foreign investors.

5   See Rules 32(2) and 37(2) of ICSID's Arbitration Rules amended with effect from 10 April 2006.

6   See, e.g., *Railroad Development Corporation v. Republic of Guatemala,* ICSID Case No. ARB/07/23.

7   See decisions available online at: <http://icsid.worldbank.org/ICSID>.

8   See, e.g., the draft rules on transparency in treaty-based investor-state arbitration currently being considered by UNCITRAL's Working Group II, available at: <http://www.uncitral.org/uncitral/commission/working_groups/2Arbitration.html>.

9   Some institutional rules contain express confidentiality provisions, such as Article 30 of the LCIA Rules and Article 34.5 of the UNCITRAL Arbitration Rules. Under Article 22(3) of the recently amended ICC Rules, the tribunal may, if requested, make orders concerning the confidentiality of the proceedings. Even absent a confidentiality provision in the applicable arbitration rules, there may be obligations of confidentiality under one or more of the laws applicable to the arbitration.

10   *Esso Australia Resources Ltd v. Plowman (Minister for Energy and Minerals)* (1995), 128 A.L.R. 391.

11   Article 11.4 of the ICC Rules.

12   Ibid.

13   Available at: <http://www.ibanet.org>.

14   See Matthias Scherer, 'The IBA Guidelines on Conflicts of Interest in International Arbitration: The First Five Years 2004-2009', in *Dispute Resolution International* 4(1) (2010) pp. 5-53.

CHAPTER TWELVE

LIABILITY OF ARBITRATION INSTITUTIONS: WHAT DOES THE FUTURE HOLD?

Teresa Cheng, SC and Justin Li

A discussion on the liability of arbitration institutions would have to start with the two decisions that have been discussed most since 2009. The first is the case of *SNF v. ICC*.[1] In the arbitration between SNF against Cytec, a series of arbitral awards were rendered in Brussels in 2002 and 2004 in which the exclusive distribution agreement between SNF and Cytec was voided on the basis that it was in breach of Article 101 of the EC Treaty. Damages in the form of loss of opportunity costs were awarded to Cytec notwithstanding the declaration of the nullity of the contract. The awards were enforced by the French Supreme Court in June 2008. In the supervisory jurisdiction, the awards were set aside by the first instance judge in Brussels in 2007. In the meantime, SNF submitted a claim against ICC on the grounds of a breach of its contractual obligations before the French courts.

In short, SNF argued that the Rules of Arbitration published by ICC were to be treated as an offer to enter into an agreement and that the arbitration clause in the exclusive distribution contract between SNF and Cytec amounted to an agreement with ICC to arbitrate under its rules. The contract between SNF and Cytec was concluded in 1993. SNF contended that the exclusion of liability provision in the 1998 ICC Rules was inapplicable since it post-dated the 1993 contract.

The contractual relationship was upheld by the Paris Court of Appeal, which held that the services provided by ICC in Paris were therefore subject to French law. The court held that the publication of the Rules of Arbitration by ICC through the International Court of Arbitration amounted to a standing offer to contract with parties that opted for an ICC arbitration clause. This contract was therefore in force when the arbitration agreement was executed, namely, in the context of this case, in 1993. As a result, the Court of Appeal held that the relevant ICC rules of arbitration should be those that were enforceable at the time of the arbitration agreement. It also added that this would be so unless the rules specifically provided that the current version of the rules enforceable on the date of the dispute should be applicable to the arbitration. Given that the 1998 Rules were in force at the time that the arbitration agreement was concluded in 1993, these would have been the applicable rules. However, the court also held that SNF and Cytec chose to submit the arbitration proceedings under the 1975 Rules for the purpose of conducting the arbitration on the grounds of the terms of reference that were signed by the parties and the members of the tribunal and explicitly referred to the 1998 Rules of Arbitration.

The 1975 ICC Rules did not contain any exclusion of liability provision, while Article 34 of the 1998 Rules provides:

> *"Neither the arbitrators, nor the Court and its members, nor the ICC and its employees, nor the ICC National Committees shall be liable to any person for any act or omission in connection with the arbitration."*

The court, while accepting that the 1998 Rules would be applicable to the conduct of the arbitration, held that ICC could not rely on the exclusion of liability clause. It held that, by reason of the contractual relationship between ICC and the parties to the arbitration, ICC was obliged to organize and administer the arbitration and to provide a structure that enabled an efficient arbitration to be conducted. It also concluded that the exclusion of liability clause, to the extent that it allowed ICC not to fulfil its essential obligations as a provider for arbitration services, must therefore be invalid. According to the court, the administrative service provided by ICC did not amount to judicial services, and the immunity prescribed under Article 34 therefore did not allow ICC to be exempted from liability. There are also other matters that were decided by the French court. The Rules of Arbitration do not impose upon ICC a duty to provide any legal opinion to any of the parties regarding requests for and advice on the legal nature of the Addendum to the Award or when an application to set aside an award would be time-barred. As to the claim that ICC did not properly scrutinize the award before issuing it, the French court made an important distinction between the role of the ICC International Court of Arbitration in scrutinizing awards, as being a non-judicial function, and the quasi-judicial role and duty conferred on the arbitral tribunal to make an award. The court further noted that the ICC Court did draw the attention to the fact that the award was susceptible to being challenged on the basis of a violation of international public policy while not interfering with the decision of the arbitral tribunal. The question whether ICC had properly controlled the arbitration proceedings was dismissed by the Court of Appeal, which pointed out that SNF (which raised the complaint) had not objected to the numerous hearings and memorials and was therefore estopped from raising the point at this late stage.[2]

In summary, the French Court of Appeal concluded that ICC had set the administrator's fees and costs correctly, had verified the time limits regarding the conduct of the arbitration and had effectively reviewed and scrutinized the award by pointing out, *inter alia*, issues of public policy that were later raised before the Belgian courts. Moreover, ICC could not be held liable for the arbitrator's reasoning. The judgment also reinforced the importance of the terms of reference in recording the agreement of the parties in adopting the 1998 Rules. The duty of ICC to properly administer its cases and to provide services for the conduct of an efficient arbitration resulting in an enforceable award was also recognized. Hence, notwithstanding Article 34 of the ICC Rules, the court opined that ICC might be liable if it failed to comply with its essential obligations as a service provider.

The duty of the arbitral institution to set the administrative fees and costs of the arbitration was also considered in a decision by the Swedish Supreme Court in December 2008.[3] The Swedish Supreme Court held that, where the seat of an arbitration is in Sweden, the Swedish courts may review the arbitrator's fees even though they may have already been set by the relevant arbitral institution, namely the Stockholm Chamber of Commerce (SCC). In this particular case, one of the parties to the arbitration challenged the award on the basis of a lack of reasoning and also sought a reduction in or reimbursement of the arbitrators' fees that had been set by SCC on the basis that they were unreasonable in the light of the work done. The Swedish court recognized that the party had a right to challenge the arbitrators' fees and costs and actually ordered costs against the three arbitrators who took part in the court action and challenged the power of the Swedish court to review their fees under the Swedish Arbitration Act. Articles 37 and 41 of the Swedish Arbitration Act empower the local courts to review the fees of the arbitrators, which have to be reasonable. This power was held to be exercisable even though the parties empowered SCC to fix the fees.

The principle that was held to be relevant by the Swedish court was ultimately not applied, as the court held that the award did not suffer from a lack of reasoning and that the arbitrators had in fact agreed to reduce their fees.

It would appear that the Swedish Supreme Court decision would only be applicable to arbitrations with its seat in Sweden. However, the power of the courts to review fees in other jurisdictions that have similar provisions in their domestic arbitration legislation may be invoked on similar grounds. Furthermore, it is not difficult to contend that the fees of arbitrators should be reasonable and that the power of the court to review the fees can therefore be invoked. Under English law, for instance, in situations where there are no agreed terms of appointment, the arbitral tribunal is to be remunerated according to reasonable rates on the basis of work done.[4] The arbitrator's normal hourly rate will then be used as the basis for calculating the fees, but the question is, of course, the number of hours that arbitrators can charge.

In *ad hoc* arbitrations, arbitrators fix their own fees. Such fees are normally included in the award and are invariably paid in advance as a form of security that is ordered by the arbitral tribunal before work is commenced. The right of the parties to challenge the "unreasonable" fees of the arbitral tribunal can be found in Section 28(2) of the English Arbitration Act, Section 77(2) of the Hong Kong Arbitration Ordinance, Section 41(2) of the Singapore Arbitration Act and Section 21(2) of the International Arbitration Act.

In another example, parties to an American Arbitration Association (AAA) arbitration sent a demand letter to AAA for the fees it paid to the sole arbitrator after her award was vacated by a US appeals court for manifest disregard of the law. The arbitration involved Richard Welshans and Deborah Williams, who entered into a franchise agreement with the US chain Coffee Beanery. The two franchisees lost in the arbitration and sought to vacate the award, contending that the arbitrator wrongly ruled that the dispute was arbitrable when it should have been referred to the courts. The Sixth Circuit set aside the award for manifest disregard of the law.[5] The franchisees claimed against AAA for the return of the arbitration fees, arguing that the fees were paid as a result of an independent obligation between the parties and the arbitrator. AAA took the position that its role was limited to collecting deposits on behalf of the arbitrator and making payments based on invoices submitted. It also relied on the limitation of liability provision in its rules for the arbitrators. In sum, AAA refused to return the arbitration fees. It appears that no action has since taken place. This exchange was revealed on a website called "Blue Mau Mau", which is a US website for franchise owners and small businesses.

Most institutional arbitration rules have a provision exempting the institution from liability. Whether that stands the scrutiny of law will no doubt depend on the national laws considering the particular provision. This raises the question what is the applicable law in construing the effect and enforceability of the exclusion of liability provisions in the rules of arbitration institutions. In the *SNF* case, the seat of arbitration is in Brussels while ICC is an entity based in France. Based on the location of the seat of the institution, the French courts decided that the applicable law would be that of France.

ICC now also has a secretariat in Hong Kong. Under the new rules that were due to enter into force on 1 January 2012, a request for arbitration can be filed in either Paris or Hong Kong. What then would be the seat of the institution if a similar question arises? Does it depend on where the request for arbitration is filed? Or should the applicable law be that of the seat of arbitration?

According to SNF, the contractual relationship established between the arbitral institution and the parties to the arbitration by entering into an arbitration agreement is in force from the date of the arbitration agreement. The source of the contractual relationship is therefore the arbitration agreement, which would normally be governed by the law of the seat of arbitration. While some observers argue that the substantive law should govern the arbitration agreement, the majority view tends to be that it should be governed by the laws of the seat of arbitration. On this basis, the applicable law for interpreting the contractual relationship and the rights and obligations arising from the arbitration agreement should be the law of the seat of arbitration rather than the law of the seat of the institution.

The China International Economic Trade Arbitration Commission (CIETAC), an arbitral institution based on the mainland of the People's Republic of China, may set up a branch/division in Hong Kong to administer arbitrations with the seat of arbitration in Hong Kong. The arbitration laws of mainland China and Hong Kong differ fundamentally. Chinese arbitration agreements are only valid if the arbitral institution is properly named in the arbitration agreement, thus precluding any ad hoc arbitration clauses. Hong Kong permits both institutional and *ad hoc* arbitration. Furthermore, the new CIETAC Rules, which are currently in their final draft form, provide that CIETAC can provide administration services under the rules of other arbitral institutions. In these complex and complicated situations, if CIETAC is to administer an arbitration under the rules of another arbitral institution, would the applicable law governing the exclusion of liability clause be that of CIETAC or the place of business of that other institution, that is to say, Chinese law or the law of the seat of that other arbitral institution? The new ICC Rules explicitly provide that the adoption of the ICC Rules would mean that the arbitral institution administering the arbitration has to be ICC. If another institution, such as the Singapore International Arbitration Centre (SIAC) or CIETAC chose to administer the ICC Rules, as has happened in the past, the question arises whether any exclusion of liability provisions would have to be construed under Singaporean, Chinese or French law.

The above-mentioned mix-and-match scenario, which is highly undesirable and, in our humble view, is not to be encouraged, poses further problems for the already difficult area of institutions' liability to arbitration users.

The final proposition may not be an unreasonable approach given that institutional rules are to be applied universally in any jurisdiction. Just as different national courts would consider the provisions in the ICC Rules in accordance with their national laws, it would probably be appropriate for the relevant institutional provisions to be considered under the laws of the seat of arbitration. However, even if this was theoretically correct, in practice a claimant would file a claim against a defendant in the defendant's jurisdiction so that its assets can be attached if the action is successful. If another action is taken against ICC, it may therefore be unavoidable that the French courts will be seized of the matter again.

In most jurisdictions, public policy would probably preclude the enforceability of exclusion of liability provisions in cases of gross negligence and certainly in the case of action or inaction arising from fraudulence or dishonesty on the part of the institution or its employees. It remains to be seen how each jurisdiction would consider whether the exclusion of liability provision exempts the institution in its discharge of what may be called the essential duties and functions of the institution.

The above-mentioned cases also draw an important distinction between the quasi-judicial functions of arbitral tribunals and the non-judicial functions of arbitral institutions. Most national arbitration laws provide for the immunity of arbitrators when exercising their quasi-judicial function in adjudicating the disputes before them. Arbitral institutions administer arbitrations. The degree of involvement of arbitral institutions differs from jurisdiction to jurisdiction. For instance, ICC provides for full and close management control of the procedures, and this is further reinforced in the new ICC Rules. On the other hand, the Hong Kong International Arbitration Centre Administered Arbitration Rules provide for what is generally described as a "light touch" approach. The HKIAC acts only as provided in the rules regarding the appointment of arbitrators and challenges against arbitrators. Its services do not include scrutiny. The pros and cons of these two types of administration are not a matter for discussion in this paper but may give rise to different expectations as to the extent of the services that the institution is meant to provide. On that basis, the structure of the exclusion of liability provision may also differ.

As seen in the *SNF* case, ICC would be expected to fix the arbitration fees as well as managing the progress of the arbitration and providing proper scrutiny of the arbitral award so as to ensure that it is enforceable. Where the arbitration rules do not provide for such services, arbitration users could probably not claim against such institutions for liability. Indeed, the level of services to be provided is usually proportionate to the level of the arbitration fees that the relevant arbitration institution charges to the users of arbitrations.

As regards ICC's duties as a service provider, the new ICC Rules have added provisions that will probably ensure that the appointment of the arbitrators is carried out in a way that suits the needs of the parties. For example, they require arbitrators to make disclosure beyond the normal conflict of interest requirements, including the number of cases that a potential arbitrator is handling. This actually makes a lot of sense, although it has attracted some criticism from arbitrators and lawyers. It would seem that the right balance would take the form of the duty of the service provider to ensure that the arbitrator it appoints or approves is in fact able to proceed with the arbitration with due diligence and reasonable dispatch. If such requests are not made of the arbitrator, it may be argued that the institution has not properly discharged its function of appointing an appropriate arbitrator on behalf of the users.

The ICC Court's practice of scrutinizing awards has since been followed by other arbitration commissions, such as SIAC and CIETAC. The scrutiny process conducted by ICC is transparent and structured. The way in which SIAC and CIETAC conduct their scrutiny processes is less transparent, as is the extent to which any liability arising from the scrutiny process may be open to discussion if the issue arises.

The over-zealous involvement of arbitral institutions in the conduct of the arbitration or in the subsequent enforcement proceedings may arguably give rise to liability of those institutions. Take the example of the *Shandong Hongri v. Petrochina*.[6] After the publication of the award, CIETAC rendered three documents at the request of the losing party, Petrochina. These documents were then produced before the enforcing court of Hong Kong. Two of the documents were from the secretariat of CIETAC and one was signed by two arbitrators. Two of these documents were produced and issued without the benefit of hearing from the winning party, Shandong Hongri. They have caused delays in the enforcement procedure and have since been scrutinized and dealt with by the Court of First Instance and the Court of Appeal. While no criticism was levied against CIETAC by the courts of Hong Kong in this particular instance, such involvement by the arbitral institution should be carefully considered. The institution's role is finished once the arbitration is concluded and the award is published. While "after-sales" service is always provided by any responsible arbitral institution, its involvement should be limited so as not to create obstacles for the winning party or to be seen to be assisting the losing party in challenging or obstructing the enforcement of the award.

Another example of the dangers of the involvement of arbitration institutions can be seen in the case of *Gao Haiyan and Another v. Keeneye Holdings Ltd and Another*,[7] in which the secretary general of the Xian Arbitration Commission was involved in the arb-med process that was conducted. Arb-med is a procedure that is acceptable and has been successfully used in Asia, in particular on the mainland and Taiwan, and arbitration institutions thus have a role to play in the dispute resolution process despite criticism of the suitability of such processes. This is not the place to discuss the pros and cons of the arb-med process, but it is important to note once again that the arbitration institution should not be involved in this process, since this is clearly a process that, provided the parties have so agreed, should be conducted by the arbitrator or arbitrators of the arbitral tribunal. While the decision in *Gao Haiyan* left much to be desired in terms of the judge's understanding of the arb-med process, and his failure to appreciate that only one of the three arbitrators was involved, it does throw some light on the extent to which an arbitration institution should—or rather should not—be involved in the dispute resolution process.

In *Gao Haiyan*, the respondent sought to set aside an order granted *ex parte* to enforce the award on the grounds of public policy, namely that the tribunal had displayed an actual or apparent bias and had relied on what was discussed at the arb-med process. During the arbitration, with the agreement of the parties, the arbitral tribunal conducted the arb-med procedure. One of the party-appointed arbitrators was assigned to carry out this task. The secretary general of the Xian Arbitration Commission participated in the arb-med process. The Court of First Instance concluded that there was apparent bias on the grounds, *inter alia*, that the figures proposed during the failed mediation were much higher than those awarded by the tribunal, that the mediation meetings were conducted over dinner and that, instead of the respondent's lawyers, a third party was approached as representing the respondent. The Court of First Instance disapproved of the fact that the secretary general had approached a third person, Zeng, instead of the respondent's lawyers. The idea of approaching Zeng came from the secretary general, who thought Zeng had influence or control over the respondent on the basis of his contacts with the parties during the early stages of the arbitration. The discussions during the mediation were reviewed by the Court of Appeal, which concluded that it could not comment on who ought to be approached and that there was evidence from Zeng that he did have some influence or control over the respondent. However, had this been a ground or a concern supported by the Court of Appeal as part of the evidence leading to the conclusion of apparent bias, the question would arise whether the Xian Arbitration Commission may be said to have assumed liability. All in all, the Court of Appeal dismissed the set-aside summons, rejected that there was anything in the arb-med process that could be said to constitute evidence of any apparent or actual basis, and enforced the award.

The secretariat of any arbitral institution provides valuable support to the arbitral tribunal in arbitrations. However, it should not be over-zealous or become involved in a way that might call the impartiality of the institution into question.

What does the future hold? Arbitration practitioners should be aware of the potential liability of the institutions that appoint them and cooperate with the secretariat in ensuring the speedy or timely resolution of cases. Institutions and arbitrators both have a duty to arbitration users to ensure a cost-effective and time-efficient resolution of the dispute. However, unscrupulous use of the potential right of arbitration users to submit claims against arbitration institutions may result in arbitration awards being improperly challenged or impaired in terms of their effects. When drafting rules, arbitration institutions will have to consider the liability that they might be exposing themselves to if the rules are attractive on paper but cannot be implemented effectively in practice. The secretariat and its staff can play a key role in the proper administration of an arbitration, and their knowledge of international practice is fundamental to the proper discharge of the functions of any arbitral institution.

The future therefore lies in the cooperation between the arbitration practitioners (legal representatives as well as arbitrators) and the arbitral institution, in order to ensure that international commercial arbitration remains the prime choice of arbitration users.

Endnotes:

1   Paris Court of Appeal, First Chamber, Section C, Case No. 07/19492, 22 January 2009.

2   This holding regarding the arbitral institution's duty to control the proceedings had in fact already been considered in previous decisions, such as: TGI Paris, *Raffineries de pétrole Homs et de Banias,* 28 March 1984, Rev. Arb. (1985); TGI Paris, *République de Guinée*, 28 January 1987, *Rev. Arb.* (1987) p. 371.

3   *Soyak International Construction and Investment Inc. v. Hober, Kraus and Melis*, No. Ö 4227-06, 3 December 2008.

4   See *K/S Norjarl A/S v. Hyundai Heavy Industries Cos Ltd,* [1983] 3 All ER 211 at 228.

5   *Coffee Beanery v. WW, LLC,* No. 07-1830, 2008 U.S. App. LEXIS 23645 (6th Cir., Nov. 14, 2008).

6   [2011] 2 HKLRD 124; [2011] 4 HKLRD 604.

7   CFI: HCCT 41/2010, unreported (12/04/2011 and 08/11/2010).

CHAPTER THIRTEEN

DEBATE: DOES EACH PLAYER MEET THE OTHERS' EXPECTATIONS? DOES THE ARBITRATION PROCESS MEET THE USERS' EXPECTATIONS?

Jean-André Diaz, Hamid Gharavi, Annette Magnusson, Pierre Tercier
Introduced by Alexis Mourre

Alexis Mourre:

I will now introduce our final panel. This panel is meant to be a debate between our four panellists and the floor. I hope it will be a vivid and controversial debate. We have here a prominent counsel, Hamid Gharavi, Partner of Derains & Gharavi; a prominent arbitrator, Pierre Tercier, who doesn't need any introduction, of course; a prominent in-house counsel, Jean-André Diaz from Total; and a prominent institutional person, and that is Annette Magnusson from the Stockholm Chamber of Commerce. The way I propose to structure this discussion is first of all to deal with three of the topics that have been addressed today. We cannot discuss all of them, because we of course do not have time for it, but I suggest that we start with those three topics that are, I believe, among the most controversial. First of all, is there a need for a code of conduct for counsel in arbitration? Do we need more guidelines, do we need more regulation? I will ask Hamid to introduce this topic in his capacity as a prominent arbitration lawyer. Hamid will introduce this topic in two or three minutes and then we will open the floor to discussion. We will do the same thing for transparency with Annette—should institutions be more transparent? Then we will discuss a question that is quite at the forefront of attention at the moment, and that is administrative secretaries, with Pierre. Once we have done that, I will ask each of the four panellists to introduce the final discussion by giving us one or two ideas on how from the perspective of counsel, in-house counsel, institutions and arbitrators—how from their perspective—we could enhance the arbitration process and make the players' interaction in arbitration more effective. I will now give the floor to Hamid. What is your view Hamid? Do we need or do we not need to regulate counsel conduct in international arbitration?

Hamid Gharavi:

Thank you Alexis for the introduction. My view as counsel is that we absolutely do not need a code of ethical conduct. Why? I would say for at least five reasons:

1) It is another document to manage. It would be the cause of abuse, possible interpretation and possible further delays and costs.

2) As a body, we are already regulated by our respective Bars. If you look at the French Bar's regulations, there is the *principe de délicatesse, de loyauté, de confraternité*. And if counsel is not happy with opposing counsel, they can have recourse to the bâtonnier, who is usually very efficient in sanctioning unethical conduct.

3) Then you have the power of the arbitral tribunal to sanction unethical conduct. We saw this morning that there is a possibility to allocate costs. Eric Schwartz said that it's sensitive, but there is also the possibility of evaluating interferences. Moreover, the *Hrvatska case* at ICSID shows that you can even exclude counsel.

4) I would be very quick in identifying the fourth reason, which is that most of the examples of unethical conduct given are due to a lack of experience or lack of judgment of counsel and that it is upon the client himself to do the diligence to hire experienced counsel with good judgment.

5) A fifth and final reason why no code is necessary is that we, as counsel, should not be blamed. Our role should not be exaggerated, we do not have the exclusivity of dilatory tactics or other issues. It's often the client that pushes for dilatory tactics. Not all clients are as sophisticated as Mr Diaz or Mr Hennessee, who spoke on this question this morning. Clients push for dilatory tactics, they push for you to challenge an arbitrator and, even when you identify the consequences of doing so, they still wish to proceed.

So for all these reasons, I beg you: no more codes.

Alexis Mourre:

Jean-André, would like to react to that? Does it all come down to the client's choice of counsel?

Jean-André Diaz:

Maybe some of the problems could come from the clients, but certainly not all of them. And this also applies to the solutions. Anyway, the question of a code of conduct is part of a larger one: do we need to regulate everything? Such a tendency exists, but is it always really necessary to have a new regulation? Concerning a code of ethics for counsel, there are already many rules, so I am not sure we need more. But some conduct has raised worries and created difficulties. It should therefore be dealt with and not forgotten. At the very least, such conduct should be placed frankly on the table and discussed constructively, even if this is not easy. An open debate is a minimum but it could help to prevent new occurrences.

Alexis Mourre:

Pierre, I am sure you will want to comment on that.

Pierre Tercier:

Volontiers. Il est usuel de rappeler que l'on se trouve dans un système pour lequel il ne faut pas trop de règles, le moins de règles possible, parce que l'arbitrage, par nature, doit être adapté à chacun. C'est vrai, mais « chassez les règles, elles reviennent au galop. »

Le fait est qu'il y en a de plus en plus. Le fait qu'il s'agisse de « soft law » est peut-être de nature à rassurer, encore qu'en l'absence d'autres normes, les directives et autres textes de ce genre tendent à recevoir une légitimité qui ne peut découler de leur seule adoption. On peut d'ailleurs se demander à quoi correspond ce besoin d'édicter des principes d'éthique pour les arbitres, pour les conseils. Toutes les professions, quelles qu'elles soient, répondent à un certain nombre de normes de comportement. Lorsqu'elles sont violées, ces normes ouvrent la voie à des actions judiciaires, par exemple en responsabilité. Le fait est que dans les domaines qui sont les nôtres, ces actions sont extrêmement rares. Ne serait-ce pas précisément en raison de cette absence de contrôle judiciaire que l'on ressent le besoin de développer des codes d'éthique ? La difficulté tient au fait que ces codes devraient effacer les différences fondamentales qui peuvent encore subsister entre les cultures juridiques, notamment sur le rôle et la fonction des conseils.

En résumé : je crois que la discussion est utile, très utile, puisqu'elle crée un véritable dialogue ; je suis en revanche plus inquiet de voir ces codes se développer s'ils contiennent des normes trop détaillées.

Alexis Mourre:

Si je comprends bien, c'est le caractère obligatoire d'un éventuel code d'éthique qui vous gêne, son côté règlementaire ?

Pierre Tercier:

Oui, c'est un code qui ne dit pas son nom. Prenons les directives IBA sur les conflits d'intérêt ou sur l'administration de la preuve dans l'arbitrage international. Tout le monde admet qu'elles ne sont pas obligatoires et qu'elles ne lient pas, tant qu'elles n'ont pas été formellement intégrées dans un accord ou un texte. Certes, mais l'on voit de plus en plus les arbitres, les conseils, quand ce ne sont pas les institutions ou les juges, s'en inspirer pour trouver une solution aisée dans des domaines souvent incertains. Sans doute est-il bon que l'on essaie de formaliser le fond commun, mais il est dangereux d'aller au-delà.

Annette Magnusson:

When it comes to the addition of new rules and guidelines on a code of ethics and so forth, I sometimes wonder if we should not be braver in the sense of leaving the detailed regulations and focusing more on the overarching values of the services that we perform. The regulations of Bar associations can be used as an example. To become a member of the Bar, there are overarching values that members of the Bar are expected to represent. The reality of commercial life is so complex that we will never be able to capture it in a set of guidelines or rules. Regardless of how detailed you make them, you will always have situations that are not addressed in the rules or guidelines, and you also risk missing the bigger picture if you stick too much to the guidelines or rules. The conflict of interest rules were mentioned here. For example, we saw in an SCC case in which an arbitrator was being challenged how in essence it was argued that the specific situation by which he was challenged was not listed in the guidelines, and therefore there was no conflict of interest. The thing is that you have to take a step back and say "what does this look like?".Is this person impartial and independent given the circumstances, even if the circumstances have not been foreseen in the rules? Does it represent a value that the arbitrator should be communicating? And in this case it did not, so this arbitrator was removed. I think it is stronger if we turn to the values that we are supposed to represent in the services that we perform, because the rules will never be able to address in full the complexity of commercial realities.

Alexis Mourre

I suggest that we now open a discussion rather than having a general Q&A session on all topics afterwards. First, on whether guidelines on counsel conduct are desirable, would anyone from the floor wish to answer?

José Rosell:

I am a strong opponent of any attempt to regulate the ethical principles applicable to counsel in a code, as Hamid said. We all have our own professional rules. The European Union has made a strong attempt to harmonize the professional rules within the European Union. They have succeeded to some extent. Why would we give a group of lawyers at the IBA, for example, the power to rule from a universal perspective on our professional rules? There is no legitimacy/or authority to overcome the laws, decrees and other regulations that are imposed on each counsel. Of course, it is not so easy in an international arbitration taking place in country A with arbitrators coming from countries B, C and D and counsel from countries E, F and G. Nevertheless, I think it would be extremely wrong to try to adopt a system whose objective would be to prevent the application to each counsel to which they are subject according to national laws and regulations. Otherwise, this would mean either that counsel should apply both rules—the Bar rules and the arbitration rules on a code of ethics, which may contradict each other—or, as suggested, that the code of ethics should override the national professional rules. For me, it doesn't make sense to give authority to an arbitral tribunal to rule on professional issues. An arbitral tribunal composed of Australian, Canadian and Bolivian lawyers trying to disqualify a firm or an attorney who is based, for example, in Paris doesn't make sense at all. The professional rules differ from one country to another. It is an excellent thing to try to harmonize the practices in arbitration, but regarding the professional rules of ethics I think that this would be a great mistake.

From the floor:

I would agree with what José just said, and I would like to add that, from my perspective, the issue whether we should have detailed rules or rather general principles, as Annette Magnusson was suggesting, has a little bit to do with the common law/civil law clash. I believe that very detailed rules bring the danger of over-regulation and also the risk of losing the flexibility that we need as arbitrators. There are no two identical situations. The more detailed the rules are, the greater the risk that we lose the ability to judge and to arbitrate properly, to put it in very simple words.

From the floor:

As a member of the disciplinary counsel of the Bar, I have experience of the fact that it is very hard to rule on the conduct and behaviour of colleagues without the authority to do so. As opposed to "ordinary" arbitration, ruling on the ethical conduct of colleagues would need some authority at least from the state, because any such ruling needs to be enforced. Many of us are not lawyers, and as we all know there is no necessity to be a member of a Bar to serve as an arbitrator or counsel in arbitral proceedings. How do we deal with this?

Isabelle Hautot:

La tendance est à l'expression de ce qui jusqu'alors était implicite – implicite parce qu'évident, et donc essentiel. L'impartialité des arbitres par exemple : l'impartialité est de l'essence même de l'acte de juger, et donc de l'œuvre de l'arbitre ; cette qualité allait donc « sans dire », - maintenant on la spécifie. Idem pour les Codes de conduite : qu'on doive « bien se comporter » et ce qu'il faut entendre par là était jusqu'alors du domaine de l'évidence - donc de l'implicite. A présent, on le spécifie. A cela d'excellentes raisons, qui tiennent essentiellement à l'extension de l'arbitrage et de la diversité des acteurs et au besoin corrélatif de clarté, si ce n'est de « transparence ». Cependant, poursuivre l'objectif, louable, que l'ensemble des règles soit d'un accès aisé pour tous quel que soit son « back ground » tend par nature à l'alourdissement et à l' « aplatissement » des règles (soit la tendance à les mettre toutes au même niveau). Avec à la clef le risque de parvenir à un résultat inverse du but poursuivi : une plus grance complexité – donc une plus grande opacité. La multiplication des Règles et Codes comporte ainsi le risque de complexifier ce qu'au départ l'on souhaite clarifier et donc simplifier. De même, l' « aplatissement » des Règles comporte le risque de banaliser l'infraction, par exemple à un Code d'Ethique, là où des règles fortes s'imposent par ailleurs aux acteurs, tels les Codes de déontologie aux avocats. C'est là, me semble-t-il, un écueil possible que tous les rédacteurs doivent conserver à l'esprit.

From the floor:

This is a difficult question, which was recently discussed in Belgium. The Brussels Bar recently issued rules allowing for contact between counsel and witnesses before the hearing. The Dutch-speaking Bar already did so 15 years ago. As a result, there were two sets of rules. In addition, we have CEPANI in Belgium, which has its own rules of conduct, which we call rules of ethics. Other institutions will probably also have their own rules. One day, ICC may have them as well. Can we go on like this? The reason for adopting such rules in Belgium is that we wanted to have equality of arms in international arbitration. As strange as it seems, it was to help the Belgian lawyers in international arbitration. That's why we adopted those rules stating that counsel can also have contact with witnesses, because under the strict rules of the Belgian jurisdictional code we normally wouldn't be able to do this. If there is a witness hearing in a court, you are not even allowed to make contact with that witness. So, rules of ethics may be helpful in promoting the Bar.

Hans van Houtte:

Most of us are convinced that ethical rules are perhaps not necessary. What is much more important is the extent to which a tribunal may effectively sanction lawyers who do not behave appropriately. Some years ago, when, as chairman, I had to file a complaint with the English Law Society against an English solicitor for intolerable behaviour, I didn't get any reply at all.

An unfortunate tactic that is used nowadays to try to derail an arbitration in which a barrister is an arbitrator is to take another barrister from the same Chambers as counsel, sometimes even just before the hearing. This may lead the other party to challenge the original barrister-arbitrator on the grounds of conflict of interest. In these circumstances, too, it would be useful if tribunals could order the party that is creating the conflict of interests by appointing the second barrister as counsel to take the latter off the case and engage another counsel.

Nayla Obeid:

It is difficult to answer this question with a simple yes or no. The answer fairly depends on how the culture of arbitration has spread in a particular country, including among counsel and arbitrators practising in the relevant jurisdictions. For example, in our region in the Middle East, we have witnessed an increasing number arbitration centres and, of course, a sharp rise in arbitration cases over the past decade, thereby denoting a wider spread of the arbitration culture in the region. We have also initiated a significant number of training sessions on arbitration with the Chartered Institute, ICC, via the PIDA seminars and through other institutions. So we cannot generalize I think. It is nonetheless true that we are, at times, faced with "guerrilla" tactics in some arbitrations, so the availability of some guidelines for counsel may prove to be useful in some jurisdictions.

Alexis Mourre:

As you can see there is plenty of room for more discussion on the topic. Now we'll move to the question of transparency. Annette would like to introduce this? Do you believe more transparency is desirable? Do we want challenge procedures with bundles and bundles of exhibits and institutional decisions that look like awards?

Annette Magnusson:

On transparency, first of all, I have two observations. I think it's interesting how investment treaty arbitration has sort of changed the landscape for all of us in terms of transparency and how the practice has developed. Investment treaty arbitration has set a standard, like it or not, for expectations on transparency in a commercial arbitration context as well. But I also think it's important to know that transparency is not something only found in international arbitration. It is a sign of the times in any line of business. So, given the opportunity and the ability, we need to have high expectations on transparency. Arbitration is not a single universe of its own. It is part of society at large, where we have increasing demands for transparency. There is a new generation of lawyers—who are now perhaps in their early twenties—with a new perception of what type of information and what access you can expect to receive from institutions and organizations. In twenty years' time, their expectations will also change the landscape of what is actually possible. So I think on the institutional side we have to follow this. We also have to become more transparent in the context of commercial arbitration.

So the next question is: how do we do this? As you know, in the field of commercial arbitration, most institutional rules, including those of the SCC, contain a confidentiality undertaking by the institutional side with respect to the parties. And we also ask this from the arbitrators. Here I think we have to focus on procedural transparency. Transparency can be transparency in the sense of opening the doors completely and making everything available. But I think that what we need to focus on from an institutional perspective is procedural transparency. What I mean by that is making it more foreseeable how the institution reaches its decisions by making our practice available. That is to day, everything that is not actually in the rules. It was noted by one of the speakers earlier today that the rules are very similar. But how are they applied in practice? There can be differences in application, and I think that is what we need to make transparent in the sense of how we apply our rules. In cases where tribunals have taken decisions on the interpretation of such rules, we should make these decisions available. And we can do this without revealing the content of the dispute or the parties involved. This is a challenge. It will not be possible to publish all disputes anonymously, because in some cases you will have to take so much out that the text no longer makes sense. However, a large proportion of decisions can be made available. I think the answer to the question whether we have to live up to more expectations on transparency from the institutional side is clearly yes, also in a commercial arbitration context.

Alexis Mourre:

Jean-André, from a user's perspective, are you happy with the ICC practice of non-reasoned decisions or would you like to see reasoned institutional decisions on challenges?

Jean-André Diaz:

Je voudrais d'abord revenir sur le mot transparence qui est très utilisé en politique et dans la presse. Il est impossible de s'opposer à un tel mot car personne ne peut dire qu'il est pour l'obscurité, l'opacité. Mais dans le domaine de l'arbitrage, il me semble que ce mot sert à couvrir deux aspects. Le premier a été évoqué dans le panel précédent : les arbitrages se déroulent au sein d'un petit monde qui pourrait permettre de cacher certains aspects suspects. Ceci est particulièrement le cas dans les arbitrages d'investissements. C'est pourquoi certains prônent l'intervention de tierces parties dans les procédures. A titre personnel, je considère qu'une telle intervention d'un tiers peut aussi présenter des difficultés car le tiers en question va inéluctablement défendre un point de vue, le sien, celui d'une partie ou encore celui d'une entité qui n'est ni partie ni intervenante sans forcément apporter plus de clarté. La deuxième façon d'aborder la transparence concerne les mécanismes d'arbitrage. Beaucoup de choses ont déjà été faites mais il est encore possible, à mon avis, de mieux faire comprendre les étapes d'un dossier particulièrement en matière de contestations relatives aux arbitres ou de révision des projets de sentence pour lesquels plus d'explications, de clarifications, donc de transparence, sont possibles. Par exemple, il pourrait être intéressant de connaître, même sur un base « neutralisée », les motifs qui ont poussé à retourner aux arbitres des projets de sentence afin qu'ils les révisent.

Alexis Mourre:
Pierre, souhaites-tu ajouter quelque-chose sur ce point?

Pierre Tercier:
Quelques mots seulement : chacun s'accorde pour admettre que la transparence est nécessaire. Je ne le conteste pas, en particulier sur l'organisation et le fonctionnement des institutions, qui mériteraient souvent d'être mieux expliqués et plus clairement révélés. Autre est la question de savoir si les décisions que prennent les institutions doivent être motivées. Le débat est connu, et il a été tout récemment à nouveau tranché par la CCI lors de la révision du règlement. A l'origine, l'idée des fondateurs de la Cour d'arbitrage était de mettre à la disposition des professionnels une institution permettant de faire rapidement avancer les procédures : cela n'est possible que si les décisions sont prises dans un délai raisonnable et qu'elles ne mettent pas en branle une procédure compliquée. La décision qui est prise reste dès lors administrative ; elle n'est pas juridictionnelle. Les parties qui acceptent cette voie s'y soumettent, parce qu'elles ont choisi l'institution, comme elles ont choisi leur arbitre. La solution peut parfois paraître dure ; elle présente sans doute ses inconvénients ; elle garantit toutefois l'objectif prioritaire : permettre à des arbitres de trancher une difficulté dans des délais raisonnables. Je regrette personnellement pour cette raison les décisions judiciaires françaises récentes qui pourraient priver la Cour d'arbitrage de la CCI d'une partie essentielle de ses compétences.

Alexis Mourre:
Hamid, you have a comment.

Hamid Gharavi:
Je suis d'accord avec tout ce qui a été dit. Je pense qu'il faut procéder au cas par cas. Ce qui est sympathique, par exemple, dans l'arbitrage d'investissement, c'est la question de l'utilité de la transparence. Son utilité se voit notamment pour la question du conflit d'intérêt : on voit quelle partie a désigné quel cabinet et quel

arbitre a été désigné. Maintenant, est-ce qu'on peut faire ça dans les arbitrages autres que les arbitrages d'investissement, sans heurter la confidentialité ? Je pense que dans une certaine mesure, oui bien entendu. On ne peut pas révéler la teneur de l'affaire ou le nom des parties, mais on peut au moins publier le numéro de l'affaire et mettre le nom du cabinet d'avocats qui intervient et les noms des arbitres. Je pense qu'il faut voir ça au cas par cas et en fonction de quels pas on peut faire vers la transparence, sans heurter la confidentialité.

Alexis Mourre:

Il faut bien distinguer la question de la transparence dans l'arbitrage d'investissement qui est en sujet et la question de la transparence dans les procédures administratives mises en œuvre par les institutions d'arbitrage, qui est un autre sujet. Et je voudrais ouvrir la discussion sur ce deuxième sujet parce qu'évidemment la question de l'arbitrage d'investissement a été beaucoup discuté et on n'a pas le temps de traiter tous les sujets mais je vais ouvrir la discussion sur ce qui est souhaitable dans l'administration des arbitrages par les institutions d'arbitrage. Est-ce que le système de la CCI ne pas motiver est un bon système ou est ce qu'il faut aller vers un système plus lourd mais plus transparent de décision motivée notamment sur les questions de récusation etc. ?

From the floor:

This is a question that can only be answered by the users of the arbitration system. If it is true, as it undoubtedly used to be, that arbitration is a private consensual process, then the clients' affairs can only be disclosed or made public to the extent to which the parties have agreed to it.

José Rosell:

J'aimerais qu'on suggère d'éviter de limiter la discussion de la transparence à la question relative à la motivation de la récusation de l'arbitre. La transparence va au-delà. J'ai souvent du mal à voir la différence entre un arbitrage entre un investisseur et un Etat dans un cadre d'un BIT ou MIT et un arbitrage commercial entre un investisseur et un Etat…C'est un sujet important qu'on a tendance à éviter dans les discussions je pense que ça vaut la peine qu'on en parle.

Karl Hennessee:

I want to take the opportunity to remind everyone that the issue of confidentiality and the issue of legal certainty are closely related in some ways. Indeed, they're usually directly connected. The more hidden the process, the less legal certainty and guidance it provides, though such certainty (especially across multiple contracts and relationships) is often a key reason for users to seek arbitration. Furthermore, confidentiality is sometimes not actually in the hands of users but in the hands of a regulatory framework to which we are all subject. Our financial reporting obligations, the dealings we have with auditors, credit rating agencies, our own internal clients and even the interest we have in maintaining consistency in legal approaches across different multinational groups can sometimes take the issue of confidentiality out of our hands. Worse yet, our own clients can try to use confidentiality (or options to breach it) as a kind of tactical weapon in order to force an opponent to undertake reporting or take a financial provision. It can be an attempt to try to force a settlement, as misguided as this may be.

Maria Vicien-Millburn:

I want to follow up on what José said in the context of commercial arbitration between states and private parties. I will not go into the question of transparency in investment treaty arbitrations. There is no dispute that a "public interest" is involved in that situation. When proceedings are instituted under a treaty against a state, it is the state that is responsible for paying the award if damages are awarded. Moreover, the dispute usually involves issues such as environmental damage, monetary policy, and so forth, which go beyond the question of the quantum that a state may be ordered to pay. This is different from a commercial arbitration between a private party and a state or an international organization. Most commercial arbitrations do not involve such a "public interest". Transparency may therefore be less essential in such cases, unless of course the parties have agreed to a transparent procedure. In the case of international organizations, confidentiality clauses are inserted into the arbitration agreement. These clauses stipulate that the arbitration is confidential but that the award can be released to the member states, for example in the event of an audit, if a member state so requests or if there is a criminal investigation and a national prosecutor requests information on the award. This would probably also apply in the case of an arbitration between a state and a private party, where the state may be under an obligation under national law to reveal certain information to the judiciary or the public.

Alexis Mourre:

We now turn to the topic of administrative secretaries, and I would like to ask Pierre Tercier to introduce it not only because he is a prominent arbitrator but also because he is Swiss and we know that the practice of secretaries first developed in Switzerland. So the question is: do we see abuses? Are we in need of more regulation of the practice? I am thinking of such abuses as delegating the tribunal's jurisdictional functions to secretaries, as well as abuses relating to costs. In ad *valorem* arbitrations, for example, agreements on the fees of the administrative secretary can be a way to circumvent the prohibition of direct fee arrangements between the arbitrators and the parties. What are your views?

Pierre Tercier:

Merci Alexis. Je n'aime pas personnellement que l'on parle d'hypocrisie car chacun sait aujourd'hui que les arbitres, à quelques très rares exceptions près que je respecte profondément, ne peuvent guère se passer de l'aide d'un ou d'une secrétaire. Il faut toutefois que les choses soient claires.

Le recours au secrétaire est pour moi pleinement justifié :

Une première remarque tient à la complexité des causes. Il est de moins en moins possible à un arbitre de maîtriser seul la quantité des documents qui lui sont soumis. Le rôle du secrétaire est alors de l'accompagner, afin de lui faciliter la tâche. L'avantage de cette solution est qu'elle permet à l'arbitre de se concentrer sur ce qui est vraiment essentiel et d'exécuter les tâches qui sont les siennes. Le rôle du secrétaire doit être en conséquence précisé : il peut suivre le dossier, établir des rapports, faire des recherches ; il est exclu en revanche pour lui de rendre la décision voire de la rédiger, même s'il n'est pas exclu pour cette dernière tâche également qu'il joue le rôle d'un assistant.

La deuxième question tient à l'aménagement de son rôle, notamment sa rémunération. Il s'agit d'une question qui peut être discutée avec les co-arbitres et les parties, avec des solutions différenciées suivant les cas (payement au forfait ou à l'heure, par exemple).

Ma troisième remarque est importante également : le recours aux secrétaires administratifs de tribunaux arbitraux permet à de jeunes juristes de gagner une expérience complémentaire, au côté des arbitres plus expérimentés. Ce n'est pas la seule école, mais c'est une bonne école.

Alexis Mourre:
A very quick reaction, Hamid. One or two minutes maximum.

Hamid Gharavi:
Je suis entièrement d'accord. Personnellement je suis soulagé en tant que conseil quand je vois un président du tribunal arbitral qui a un secrétaire administratif. Généralement, ça se passe mieux.

Annette Magnusson:
First, in SCC practice, when secretaries are used by the tribunals, we ask the tribunal to channel this question to the parties through the SCC secretariat. So the secretariat effectively asks the parties whether or not they agree to the appointment of an administrative secretary. And second, the fees of the secretary are drawn from the fees of the arbitrator. So, in fact, the costs of the tribunal will not increase when they use a secretary. The cost of the arbitration will be the same for the parties.

Jean-André Diaz:
C'est un sujet sur lequel j'ai envie de poser une question plutôt de donner une réponse : je voudrais savoir s'il y a des cas où un secrétaire a été refusé quand un président l'a demandé? On me dit à l'instant que oui, c'est déjà un élément qui devrait être souligné. Du point de vue d'une entreprise, d'une partie, il ne faut pas oublier l'aspect coût. On demande toujours à un juriste d'entreprise de chiffrer le coût d'un arbitrage. Pour les institutions, grâce aux barèmes, il est assez facile de déterminer le coût d'un arbitrage (en plus des honoraires des conseils) et ce chiffre est pris en compte dès le début. Quand arrive ultérieurement une demande d'un secrétaire pour le Tribunal arbitral ou son Président, le juriste d'entreprise est plus gêné puisque la procédure a déjà commencé. Il vaudrait mieux que cet aspect soit évoqué et tranché dès le début.

Alexis Mourre:

Thank you. We will now conclude the debate. I will ask each of our panellists to give us, in no more than one minute, one idea and one suggestion on how to improve the interaction between the various arbitration players. Hamid, would you like to start?

Hamid Gharavi:

Yes, with pleasure. I would encourage clients to move quickly. They should provide us with the documents on time. In some case, the main reason why counsel is late is that we do not receive the materials in time. For arbitrators, the question of availability is important. I know that we have talked about it, but it's not because we have talked about it that it has been resolved. I just want to praise Professor Tercier, whom we approach as president and who always says *"tu ne me fais pas un « sale coup, » ce n'est pas un gros dossier de construction j'espère ? Une partie n'est pas en train de demander de mesure provisoire ?»*. On pose les bonnes questions pour voir si on est disponible avant d'accepter. Finalement, l'administration. Je prends l'exemple de la CCI. On peut parfois être déçu par son rôle passif. Je vous donne un exemple très rapidement. Récemment une partie n'a pas payé ses frais d'arbitrage à temps – de son côté la CCI attend comme un robot. La partie défaillante ne se manifeste pas. La CCI écrit à l'autre partie pour lui demander de se substituer, sans même inviter la partie défaillante à clarifier sa position ou vérifier qu'il ne s'agisse pas d'un oubli, etc. On envoie une lettre à la CCI en l'invitant au moins à demander des clarifications à la partie défaillante pour s'assurer que ce n'est pas une omission ou que c'est effectivement parce qu'elle ne veut pas payer. La CCI nous répond que ce n'est pas son rôle de demander des clarifications et invite notre client à se substituer à la partie défaillante en payant sa part des frais de l'arbitrage. En tant qu'usager, on attend un rôle autre de la part des administrations d'arbitrage.

Annette Magnusson:

How do we enhance the arbitration process? This is the million dollar question, but I think each player must play its part. On the institutional side, we must continue to do our utmost to appoint the right person for each specific case, but we also need to follow the performance more closely. This is a difficult task in terms of getting feedback from the users and the arbitrators on the conduct of the proceedings. But the appointment is one of the most important things that we do as an institution. It has great implications for the continuation of the process. We need to work closely with the arbitrators in a dialogue. How we as an institution can help the arbitrators to conduct the case in an efficient and professional manner. To assist the arbitrators in that respect. And when it comes to other players, the parties and counsel, I think the answer to many of the challenges of international arbitration that we are discussing today, in particular those related to the issues of time and costs, lies in the relationship between client and counsel. It strikes me that there seems to be a lack of dialogue at times. Counsel need to understand the business objectives of the clients, and clients need to be clear on what their business objectives are in a particular dispute. Earlier today we heard that if a long-term relationship is at stake in the arbitration, this influences the way you expect the arbitration to be conducted. I think this type of conversation is very important. From my perspective, I think that client and counsel can probably do more to start talking to one another.

Pierre Tercier:

Dans cette perspective, j'aime beaucoup le thème choisi pour cet événement. La responsabilité de la qualité des procédures et surtout de la qualité des sentences incombe fondamentalement aux arbitres. Mais ils n'en sont pas les seuls garants, pas plus que les professeurs d'université ne sont garants des résultats de tous leurs élèves. La qualité des procédures et des sentences dépend aussi fondamentalement de la qualité des conseils et de leurs écritures. C'est pourquoi je suis convaincu de la nécessité de créer un climat de collaboration, entre les arbitres d'une part, mais aussi entre les parties, les conseils et les institutions, sans parler des juges dont le rôle correcteur et directeur est essentiel. Le président du tribunal arbitral joue dans cette mesure un rôle central. C'est lui qui donne le style, c'est lui qui crée le climat; c'est lui qui doit pouvoir obtenir de chacun la meilleure contribution.

Jean-André Diaz:

Pour reprendre dans une certaine mesure ce que vient de dire le Professeur Pierre Tercier, il ne faut pas oublier que l'arbitrage n'est pas quelque chose d'acquis, d'inéluctable. Même si les clauses d'arbitrage sont effectivement souvent examinées dans les derniers moments d'une négociation, il faut rappeler qu'il faut souvent se battre pour les faire accepter. Sans ces efforts, il n'y aurait pas de clauses d'arbitrage ni d'arbitrages car le recours aux juges étatiques est toujours possible à défaut d'autres dispositions. A cet égard, je voudrais rappeler que les juristes d'entreprises sont de réels promoteurs de l'arbitrage. Ce matin j'ai été un peu surpris d'entendre parler de désengagement des entreprises et donc de leurs juristes. Certes il y a des entreprises qui n'ont pas de juristes ou qui en ont peu, souvent alors absorbés par la vie économique courante, et qui s'en remettent donc entièrement à leurs conseils externes. Mais il y a quand même beaucoup d'entreprises, et bien sûr parmi celles-ci les plus grandes, qui sont au contraire fortement engagées en matière d'arbitrage et qui y accordent une grande importance. C'est d'ailleurs une des raisons qui ont poussé un certain nombre de juristes d'entreprise à créer le Corporate Counsel International Arbitration Group (CCIAG) et je peux vous assurer que ces juristes sont très impliqués et participent à toutes les étapes, à toutes les audiences des arbitrages. On est donc loin d'un désengagement. Pour revenir en conclusion sur la question sous-jacente de nos travaux : peut-on progresser par plus de réglementation, je n'en suis pas toujours sûr, mais je reste convaincu que l'on peut progresser par plus d'explication.

Alexis Mourre:

Thank you. This brings us to a close of the final panel, and of course the final words belong to our chairman, Yves Derains.

Yves Derains:

Il m'appartient de conclure cette réunion annuelle de l'institut qui, je crois, nous a apporté beaucoup d'enseignements. Je note d'abord, comme l'a relevé Pierre

Tercier qu'il y a une continuation directe entre nos débats d'aujourd'hui et nos débats de l'année dernière, qui portaient sur le sujet « tant vaut l'arbitre tant vaut l'arbitrage » et qui a donné lieu à la publication que vous avez à peu près tous. Je ne veux pas parler longtemps, car tout le monde a envie de participer à la remise de prix qui va suivre. Je voudrais simplement dire que les discussions d'aujourd'hui m'amènent à deux réflexions. On avait dit l'année dernière « tant vaut l'arbitre, tant vaut l'arbitrage, ». Cette année nous parlons de l'interaction des acteurs dans l'arbitrage international et je dirais que tant valent les acteurs tant vaut l'interaction. Ce matin et cette après-midi, mais surtout ce matin, on a envisagé 2 types d'interactions : l'interaction entre les conseils, les arbitres et les entreprises et ensuite l'interaction entre les arbitres, les conseils et les institutions. Et évidemment, c'est dans ces interactions qu'il peut, comme on l'a montré à maintes reprises, y avoir de bons et de mauvais résultats. Mais il y a une tendance qui me parait extrêmement dangereuse et que j'ai perçue chez certains intervenants. C'est d'essayer de faire peser les mauvais résultats soit sur les conseils dans l'interaction arbitre – client, soit sur les arbitres dans l'interaction institution- conseil - client. Je pense que c'est vraiment une fausse approche et que l'idée, par exemple, qui consiste à dire que la présence des clients devrait etre obligatoire aux audiences parce qu'en leur absence on ne sait pas ce que les conseils peuvent faire me parait une approche assez déraisonnable. De même laisser entendre que le rôle des institutions serait essentiellement de contrôler les arbitres pour qu'ils ne se livrent pas à un comportement répréhensible, est encore une approche erronée. Dans les le premier cas on n'oublie totalement la responsabilité des entreprises dans le choix des conseils. Dans le second, il ne faut pas mettre en question le fonctionnement d'une institution parce qu'il y a de mauvais choix ont été exercés. Et je crois qu' Isabelle Hautot ce matin a très bien expliqué que le conseil et le client travaillent en étroite coopération. L'idée que la présence du client à l'audience serait indispensable pour empêcher le conseil de faire des bêtises me parait bien puérile. Même chose dans l'interaction institution - client - arbitre ou conseil – arbitre. Dans ce cas-là, si l'on attend des institutions qu'elles contrôlent les arbitres pour les empêcher de se consacrer à des activités à la limite du répréhensible, il faut remettre en cause le choix de ces arbitres par l'institution. Penser que les arbitres vont essayer de gratter un peu d'argent sur ceci ou sur cela, de tripler leur frais de photocopies alors que l'on leur confie des dossiers qui portent sur des millions et des millions de dollars, n'est pas rationel. Là encore il faut que les institutions prennent la responsabilité de nommer des bons arbitres. Par ailleurs, je crois qu'il y a un danger dans une vision uniformisante de l'arbitrage. L'arbitrage international n'est pas une entité à facette unique. Aussi, lorsque l'on aborde la question par des codes, par des règles générales, on oublie ce caractère. Dans tous les pays du monde, l'arbitrage a des caractéristiques qui lui sont propres. Plus que des caractéristiques qui viendraient de la loi ou du droit même, ce sont des caractéristiques culturelles. Etablir un code sur la conduite des avocats qui s'appliquerait aussi bien à un arbitrage entre un avocat salvadorien et un avocat argentin au Costa Rica qu'à un arbitrage entre un avocat suédois et un avocat américain à Londres serait totalement artificiel. Les attentes ne sont pas les mêmes dans chacun de ces arbitrages et partir d'un code unique pour ensuite envisager les sanctions que pourrait prendre l'arbitre le serait encore plus car l'arbitre risquerait de prendre des sanctions ne correspondant absolument pas aux attentes des parties. Il faut tenir compte et même favoriser la diversité de l'arbitrage car, comme on l'a dit, l'arbitrage est avant tout ce que les parties veulent qu'il soit et les parties ne veulent pas toutes ni tout le temps la même chose. En fin, et je terminerai la dessus, s'il y a une préoccupation commune, comme quelqu'un d'autre l'a également dit, c'est de faire que l'arbitrage se déroule bien. C'est à l'aune de cette préoccupation des uns et des autres que l'on doit donner un certain nombre de pouvoirs aux arbitres. On parlait de la sanction que peut prendre un arbitre vis-à-vis de tel avocat qui ne respecte pas telle ou telle règle déontologique. Personnellement je ne pense pas que l'arbitre soit là pour faire respecter des règles déontologiques quelles qu'elles soient, mais qu'en revanche il est là pour faire respecter l'égalité des parties dans l'arbitrage, et faire en sorte que l'égalité des armes soit une réalité. C'est par ce biais qu'il peut sanctionner un avocat. Ce n'est pas parce que l'avocat aurait violé les règles du barreau de Bruxelles ou d'ailleurs, c'est parce que compte tenu de sa situation particulière dans l'arbitrage il bénéficie d'atouts que n'a pas l'autre partie. Ce déséquilibre donne à l'arbitre les pouvoirs de rétablir l'équilibre, si nécessaire en faisant exclure cet avocat de l'arbitrage. Ce faisant, il n'applique pas des règles déontologiques particulières. Il fait en sorte que les règles propres à la procédure de l'arbitrage soient respectées.

J'ai beaucoup trop parlé. Je voudrais remercier tout le monde, bien entendu tous ceux qui sont intervenus comme orateurs, ceux qui ont posé des questions, ceux qui ont eu la patience d'écouter sans même poser de question, remercier aussi nos interprètes qui ont fait un excellent travail. Donc merci à tous et je déclare cette réunion close, pour ouvrir immédiatement la cérémonie d'attribution du prix de l'Institut.

CONCLUDING REMARKS

Alexis Mourre

Is arbitration really dysfunctional, as posited by some? Are the parties' expectations deceived? Who bears responsibility? Is there need for sweeping reforms? Should arbitration as a private system of adjudication be regulated? To what extent can institutions fix the problems of time and costs in arbitration?

These are the difficult and complex questions that were discussed today. Of course, no one expected solutions to appear suddenly, for there is no magical recipe that could all of a sudden resolve all the perceived problems of international arbitration. But we have debated the contemporary problems of arbitration from a practical perspective, as we always do at the Institute, and we have done so in a balanced way, bearing in mind the expectations of the users – which may not all be legitimate or realistic – and the inherent constraints of any jurisdictional activity. Undoubtedly, arbitration is facing a number of challenges. As a private system of adjudication, it has reached maturity, and as any mature industry, it needs to renew itself. Arbitration needs to look at the future, and it probably cannot do so without going back to the basics. All of us acknowledge the difficulties that arbitrators and parties sometimes encounter. Arbitration has become more complex. It takes more time. It is costly. Arbitrators are sometimes overburdened. They are too often insufficiently organized, faced to large teams of counsels who will flood them with what Michael Schneider once described as the paper tsunami - thousands of pages of submissions and hundreds of thousands of pages of evidence. Those problems are real, albeit hardly new. Whether and to what extent they have worsened in recent years can be debated. What has certainly increased exponentially is the number of articles, seminars, and the overall level of communication dedicated to these questions, to the point that one could wonder whether part of the climate of crisis that has developed in arbitration is not due to a certain level of self-inflicting anti-arbitration propaganda.

If anything, this conference will have contributed to dispel certain misconceptions. One such misconception is the idea that the time and costs of arbitration are ultimately attributable to the greed of busy arbitrators pursuing their own private commercial interest by piling up cases and delaying the solution of disputes. Such idea fails to acknowledge that more than 80% of such costs relate to the parties' own defense and representation by counsel of their own choice; and as Bernard Hanotiau noted, arbitrators are often faced with requests for postponements that can generate important delays. Another misconceived idea is that counsel and clients would have diverging interests, with counsel wanting to encourage long and complex procedures to inflate their own fees, hence the suggestion that the personal presence of their clients at the hearings should be made mandatory in order to ensure that they will not misbehave. The "whose fault is it?" approach is certainly not the proper way to deal with the contemporary challenges that international arbitration if facing.

The regulatory approach is equally misconceived. We now hear more and more voices advocating a regulatory upheaval of arbitration, which would consist in introducing rules forbidding unilateral appointments, generalizing rosters and separating the roles of counsel and arbitrator, not only in investment arbitration, but also in commercial arbitration. This would pave the way to the transformation of arbitration from a private system of adjudication into some sort of a global administrative justice, with unpredictable and far reaching consequences. The system would become closer to court litigation, with the emergence of a new generation of arbitrators who would depend more from arbitral institutions and their politics and less from the market. No one has to gain from such an evolution.

The challenges facing arbitration are however real, and they need to be addressed in a manner that is consistent with the private and consensual nature of this private system of dispute resolution. The bottom line is that parties freely choose their counsel, they freely select, based on the different rules offered by each institution, the institutional rules they want to submit to. And they freely select their arbitrators, who are private practitioners competing one against the others in a free and opened market. Because parties are free to choose their counsel, their arbitral institution and their counsel, they can and should move away from the counsels, institutions and arbitrators who they believe have been inefficient or dysfunctional and encourage more efficient ones, including new comers. The real question is another: how to make the interaction between good counsel, good institutions and good arbitrators optimal?

Arbitration, at the difference of court litigation, supposes a minimum level of bona fide cooperation between arbitrators and parties. Arbitrators sometimes forget that they provide a service to the parties, while the parties do not always bear in mind that advocacy in arbitration is different from court litigation.

As rightly pointed out this morning by Bernard Hanotiau, arbitration advocacy tends to become more and more sophisticated. In complex cases, the volume of memorials and evidence received by arbitrators has increased notably. And, in a maybe more worrisome fashion, there seems to be a reflex phenomenon in smaller and less complex cases, where an often disproportionate level of advocacy is deployed by counsel, with the result of making the ratio costs/amount is dispute unsustainable. Part of this trend is probably due to the fear by counsel of the liability that might arise if it fails to argue any and all possible argument in favor of its client, and to the fear by arbitrators of annulments based on their failure to respond in their award to argument raised by one of the parties, even if entirely immaterial to the outcome. Shorter and more focused submissions would certainly help to make arbitration speeder, less costly and more efficient. This would suppose that arbitrators could more easily give directions to the parties, not only at the outset of the arbitration but all along the proceedings, by informing them of their provisional views and of the issues they believe relevant. Too often, however, arbitrators refrain from doing so by fear of being challenged. Equally, the inflating concept of procedural public policy and the fear of annulments on due process grounds leads to a significant increase of the time of the arbitration by multiplying the number of submissions until when all parties will have had a full opportunity to respond to any and all of the arguments raised by the others, irrespective of their relevance and materiality. We should think of ways to permit arbitrators to narrow the issues they believe relevant and material and to consequently focus and limit the submissions and the evidence. Part of the solution to this problem probably lies in less court interference and more discretion in favor of arbitrators in the conduct of the proceedings.

Another aspect of the solution is avoiding that arbitrators and institutions be taken hostages of dissatisfied parties by instrumental liability actions. We have seen in recent months some egregious examples of such unacceptable tactics. The problem is twofold. First, there should be a clear rule of immunity in favor of arbitrators and institutions. From this standpoint, decisions such as that rendered by the Court of appeals of Paris in the SNF vs. CCI case are unhelpful. Arbitrators should also enjoy better insurance coverage, in particular with respect to their representation costs. Second, there should be a clear choice-of-court rule – for example in institutional rules or in terms of reference – allowing arbitrators to know where – possibly at the seat - disputes with respect to their liability would take place.

Another pervading question is, finally, that of the tools available to arbitrators to efficiently manage the proceedings. More often than not, the volume of documentation submitted and the complexity of the issues involved makes it extremely difficult for the arbitrators to manage the proceedings and issue the award in a reasonable time without the help of a secretary, in the same way as clerks to justices are used in many fora. As Constantine Partasides rightly noted, most of the objections advanced against the use of secretaries are misplaced. This is of course not to say that the use of secretaries should not be monitored by institutions in order to avoid that arbitrators will improperly delegate their decision-making functions. But the proper use of secretaries in assisting the arbitrators in their analysis of the evidence and arguments and in the preparation of certain portions of the draft award will certainly help them in timely making quality awards.

Many other areas of practice will need to evolve in order to address the problems and challenges of contemporary international arbitration. It is our hope that this conference and the ensuing Dossiers of the Institute will have contributed to the reflection and paved the way to pragmatic and efficient solutions that will be consistent with the consensual nature of this private system of international adjudication.

INDEX

A

AAA International Arbitration Rules..56 n. 46

AAA/ABA Code of Ethics for Arbitrators in Commercial Disputes....................54, 56

ABA Model Rules of Professional Conduct..28

ACICA Arbitration Rules [Australia] ....56 n. 46

administered arbitration
arguments in favour of 105

American Arbitration Association (AAA) 123-124

amiables compositeurs.. 54

amicus briefs 114

arbitral awards
as guides to contracts...47
deadlines for..107
drafting of.. 78-79, 79-80, 90-91
speed v. reasoning.. 47

arbitral institutions
and secretaries to arbitral tribunals 109-110
duties of
facilitating swift appointment of tribunal....................107-108, 126
handling challenges against arbitrators................................108-109
monitoring timetable 108
scrutinizing and issuing awards.....................................109, 117, 126
setting and collecting fees.. 109, 123-124, 126
sharing information with arbitrators 108
involvement in arbitral procedure......................... 100-101, 102, 125-127
liability of
see liability

remuneration method and scales...101
successful interaction with parties and tribunals 102-103
suitability for international arbitration 100

arbitral tribunal
chairman
        see president of the arbitral tribunal
president
        see president of the arbitral tribunal
secretaries
        see secretaries to arbitral tribunals

arbitration
improving interaction between players in 102-103, 142-143
institutional v. ad hoc...99-100
objective of.. 9

Arbitration Act 1996 [UK] 36
section 2 ....62 n. 70
section 20 ....82 n. 15, 83 nn. 17 & 18
section 28 123
section 29 ....58, 59 n. 62, 94, 97 n. 9
section 33 ....52, 54, 55, 56
section 34 ....52, 84 n. 24
section 63 39
section 65 39

arbitrators
appointment/selection of..................................... 51-52, 107-108, 115-116
challenges against 55, 108-109, 116-117
duties towards institutions..107
duties towards parties
        conducting arbitration fairly and without undue delay.............16-17, 56, 106
        confidentiality 56-57
        considering own availability.. 106
        delivering an award within a reasonable time 107
        delivering an enforceable award.. 57
        determining the dispute 53-54

impartiality and independence.............................. 17-18, 54-55, 105-106

expectations of..49

immunity of

    see immunity

intimidation of...59-60

involvement in cross-examination......................................12-13

liability of

    see liability

powers 53-54, 57-58, 62

removal of..36-37, 55, 106, 108-109

remuneration of..58, 101

resignation of 61-62, 95

rights

    free decision-making... 59-61

    immunity from suit...59, 93-96

    non-interference in the decision-making process 60

    protection against vexatious conduct 59-60

    remuneration 58-59

    right to dissent... 61

    right to resign 61-62

    secrecy of deliberations 61

rights v. powers 57-58, 62

sanctions available to... 16-17

shift of power from parties to... 50

source of mandate

    applicable arbitration law.. 52

    arbitration agreement 50-51

    arbitration rules 51

    other law governing arbitration.................................. 52-53

    terms of appointment 51-52

testimony... 56, 57

arbitrator's contract

as a contract for services .... 51 n. 5

as a sui generis contract 51

as an agency contract... 51 n. 4

express or implied .... 50-51 arb-med procedure.. 127

B

bad faith.. 95-96

Belgian Judicial Code
art. 1689...62 n. 74
art. 1696...84 n. 24
art. 1701..82
n. 15, 83 n. 18
art. 1702...57 n. 53

Bilateral Investment Treaties (BITs)..99

C

CAM Rules [Italy]
art. 8..56 n. 46
art. 20..73 n. 28
art. 25..84 n. 26

CAMCA Arbitration Rules ....56 n. 46

CCBE Code of Conduct for European Lawyers
art. 1..20 n. 1
art. 4..10, 20
n. 2

CEPANI [Belgium]... 135

China International Economic Trade Arbitration Commission (CIETAC)... 124-125,
126-127

CIETAC Rules [China]...56 n. 46

clients
see users

Code of Conduct for the Bar of Ireland ....33 n. 33

confidentiality

see also transparency

in document production 16-17, 30

of awards 115

of deliberations 61, 71

provisions in arbitration rules on 114

Convention on the Settlement of Investment Disputes between
States and Nationals of Other States (Washington Convention) 94

cost-capping 38-39

counsel

duties

relating to document production

see document production

to advocate in good faith 14

to be properly equipped and trained.. 11-13

to be properly prepared.. 11-13

towards tribunal and parties 9-10, 18

exclusion of...17-18

improper conduct

applicable laws...16-17

as strategy or tactic.. 14-15, 18

due to lack of experience/preparation..11-13

lack of detailed standards regarding 11, 19

tribunal's jurisdiction over.. 16-17, 30-31

integrity of... 15

need for ethical standards of conduct for..24-26, 132-136

relationship between in-house and external counsel 46

Court of Arbitration for Sport (CAS) Code

art. 44...82 n. 14

arts. 46 & 59 ....83 n. 18

cross-examination

of experts..12-13

of witnesses 12, 14-15

D

deadlines 56

delegation of powers 72-73, 79-80, 87-91

Departmental Advisory Committee on Arbitration Law (DAC) Report 39, 52, 62

depositions .... 13, 21 n. 11

devil's advocate 78

disclosure
see document production

dissent 61

document production
common law v. civil law 26-27
different national practices 23-24
duty of candour 29
duty of confidentiality 16-17, 30
duty of diligence 27-29
ethical standards for 27-30
tribunal's role in .... 13, 14, 20 n. 9, 26

Dutch Code of Civil Procedure
art. 1029 .... 62 n. 74
art. 1039 .... 84 n. 26
art. 1051 .... 82 n. 15

E

European Convention on Human Rights .... 22 n. 25, 55

evidence
see also document production
exclusion of 17
spoliation of 15

taking of.. 73

ex aequo et bono 54

experts 12-13

F

Federal Arbitration Act [US] 56

Federal Rules of Civil Procedure [US] 13, 28-29

FIDIC Conditions of Contract... 36

French Code of Civil Procedure
art. 1467... 73, 84 n. 27
art. 1479..83 n. 16
art. 1513..83 n. 18

French Decree no. 2011-48 of 13 January 2011 ....62 n. 72

G

German Code of Civil Procedure (ZPO)
art. 1038...62 n. 73
art. 1042(4)...84 n. 24
art. 1052(1)...82 n. 18
art. 1052(2)...82 n. 15

German Institute of Arbitration (DIS)...100-101

German Institute of Arbitration (DIS) Rules....................................82 n. 11

H

Hong Kong Arbitration Ordinance 123

Hong Kong International Arbitration Centre (HKIAC) 125-126

I

IBA General Principles for the Legal Profession ....10, 15 n. 13

IBA Guidelines on Conflicts of Interest in International Arbitration ....
55, 55 n. 36, 117

IBA International Code of Ethics ....10, 20 n. 3

IBA Rules of Ethics for International Arbitrators .... 56, 83 n. 16

IBA Rules on the Taking of Evidence in International Arbitration..........14 n. 10, 27,
63 n. 15

ICC Court of Arbitration 100, 102, 116,
117, 121-122, 126

ICC Note on the Appointment of Administrative Secretaries........................... 89-90

ICC Rules of Arbitration
art. 11 ....106, 106
n. 2, 116 n. 11
art. 12 .... 67, 108
art. 14 109
art. 15 (1998) .... 16, 17 n. 15
art. 15 (2012) .... 73 n. 28, 79 n. 41
art. 21 ....54 n. 20
art. 22 ....17 n. 15, 53, 72, 106 n. 2, 114 n. 9
art. 23 ....107 n. 3
art. 24 ....107 n. 3
art. 25 53
art. 29 108
art. 30 56
art. 31 ....83 n. 18
art. 33 109
art. 34 122
art. 36 109
art. 40 59
art. 41 110

appendix IV 72

ICDR Guidelines for Arbitrators Concerning Exchanges of Information ..... 20 n. 9

ICSID Convention
art. 44 .... 21 n. 22
art. 48 61
art. 52 18
art. 56 18

ICSID Rules of Arbitration 18
art. 6 .... 65 n. 47
art. 14 .... 70, 82 n. 10
art. 15 .... 83 n. 16
art. 16 .... 70 n. 13, 83 n. 18
art. 32 .... 114 n. 5
art. 37 .... 114 n. 5
art. 46 .... 66 n. 69

immunity
and (gross) negligence 94-95, 95-96
and fraud and wrongdoing 94, 95-96
and role of arbitrators 94
as a right of arbitrators 59, 93-96
rationale for 93-94

impartiality 17-18, 54-55, 78, 93-94, 105-106

Indonesia 59-60

in-house counsel
see counsel
see users

International Centre for Settlement of Investment Disputes (ICSID) 100, 101, 113-114

Iran-US Claims Tribunal Rules of Procedure 61

Italian Code of Civil Procedure
art. 816-ter .... 73, 84 n. 26
art. 823 .... 82 n. 15, 83 n. 18

iura novit curia 54

K

KLRCA Rules [Malaysia] .... 56 n. 46

L

LCIA Court .... 55, 100, 101, 108 n. 5, 109, 110, 117

LCIA India Rules .... 106 n. 1

LCIA Rules of Arbitration
art. 9 108
art. 10 106
art. 13 .... 107 n. 3
art. 14 .... 41 n. 4, 53, 82 n. 11, 83 n. 17, 106
art. 24 107
art. 26 .... 83 nn. 17 & 18
art. 30 .... 56 n. 46, 61, 114 n. 9
art. 31 59
art. 32 110

liability
see also immunity
of arbitral institutions
    applicable law 124-125
    as opposed to tribunals 125-126
    exclusion clauses 121-122, 125
    in the future 128
    regarding fees 123-124, 126
    regarding involvement in arbitration procedure 126-127
    regarding services 122, 125-126
of arbitrators 59, 93-96, 95-96, 125-126, 128

LMAA Intermediate Claims Procedure 39, 40

LMAA Small Claims Procedure 38

M

money-laundering.. 57

N

New York Convention on the Recognition
and Enforcement of Foreign Arbitral Awards.. 56

(gross) negligence 94-95, 95-96, 125

NAFTA.. 113

O

oral hearings...37-38

P

parties
see also users
expectations of.. 49
freedom to select counsel... 18
rights of... 56
shift of power to arbitrators 50

Permanent Court of Arbitration (PCA) 99, 100, 101

pre-hearing conference 70

president of the arbitral tribunal
delegated powers
    general...72
    regarding the taking of evidence..73
    regarding time management 72-73

implied powers
      casting vote 71
      chairing hearings 70
      contacts with parties 69
      deciding hearing related matters 69
      general...68
      organizing deliberations..71
      representing full tribunal 70
      setting time limits 69
      signing procedural orders alone 69-70
lack of rules regarding..67
nature of role.. 67, 68, 72, 74
relationship with co-arbitrators 76-80
relationship with parties..74-76

R

Rules of Arbitration of the Court of
International Commercial Arbitration [Romania] ....56 n. 46

S

SCC Arbitration Institute [Sweden]..100, 101, 123

SCC Rules [Sweden]
art. 13..107-108
art. 16..83 n. 18
art. 17..73 n. 28

secrecy
see confidentiality

secretaries to arbitral tribunals
accommodation in UNCITRAL Rules of Arbitration 88-89
allocation of costs for..91
and arbitral institutions 109-110
appropriate role...89-91
arguments against using...88
background 87

duties of.. 90-91
recent developments regarding.. 88-89
regulation of..140-141

self-policing 25

Sewage Farm case 35-36

SIAC Rules [Singapore]
art. 5 108
art. 10 106
art. 14 ....106, 108
art. 16 ....106 n. 2
art. 28 ....107, 109
art. 30 109
art. 36 110

Singapore Arbitration Act 123

Singapore International Arbitration Centre (SIAC) 125, 126

Spanish Arbitration Law... 94, 97 n. 10

submarine client 43

Swedish Arbitration Act .... 83 n. 18, 123

Swiss Arbitration Association 100, 101

Swiss Private International Law Act (PILA)....................73, 83 n. 18

Swiss Rules of International Arbitration
art. 14..73 n. 28
art. 31..82 nn. 11 & 12, 83 nn. 17 & 18
art. 43..56 n. 46, 83 n. 16

T

Techniques for Controlling Time and Costs in Arbitration ....84 n. 22

time management.. 70, 71, 72-73

transparency
arguments for and against...115, 118, 136-140
challenges to arbitrators...116-117
in commercial arbitration...114-115
in investment arbitration... 114
scrutiny and amendment of draft awards 117-118
selection of arbitrators..115-116

U

unanimity...77

UNCITRAL Model Law .... 39, 56, 59, 83 n. 18, 106

UNCITRAL Notes on Organizing Arbitral Proceedings..89

UNCITRAL Rules of Arbitration 30, 99, 101
art. 5...89
art. 15...73 n. 28
art. 16...89
art. 17... 54 n. 18, 106
art. 27...53
art. 33..82 nn. 11 & 12, 83 nn. 17 & 18
art. 34... 114 n. 9
art. 35... 54 n. 20
art. 40...89

Uniform Arbitration Act [US] ....20 n. 9

urgency..69, 70, 108

users
appointment as arbitrators...35-36

communication with external counsel...43

involvement in proceedings of..43-44, 45-46

involvement in strategy and tactics 44-45

role in determination of costs..38-39

role in drafting arbitration agreements 37

role in oral hearings...37-38

shared interests with counsel 36-37

US-style discovery ....13, 14, 20 n. 9, 26

V

Venezuelan Code of Civil Procedure 28

Vienna International Arbitral Centre (VIAC).................................100, 101

W

Washington, George 54-55

witnesses 12, 14-15

World Intellectual Property Organization (WIPO) Arbitration Rules ....56 n. 46

X

Xian Arbitration Commission [China] 127

TABLE OF CASES

Amco Asia Corp., US and Others v. Republic of Indonesia [ICSID] ....60 n. 67

Azran v. Schirer, Leclercq, Nahum and the Company SAS Consultaudit [France] 95-96

Biwater Gauff (Tanzania) Ltd v. United Republic of Tanzania [ICSID] 60

Cementownia "Nowa Huta" SA v. Turkey [ICSID] 30

CME v. Czech Republic [Sweden] ....56 n. 51

Coffee Beanery v. WW, LLC [US] 123-124

Esso Australia Resources Ltd v. Plowman (Minister for Energy and Minerals) [Australia] 114

Gao Haiyan and Another v. Keeneye Holdings Ltd and Another [Hong Kong]...127

Generation Ukraine, Inc. v. Ukraine [ICSID] 29

Himpurna California Energy Ltd v. Republic of Indonesia [UNCITRAL]...........56 n. 50, 59-60

Hrvatska Elektroprivreda d.d. v. Republic of Slovenia [ICSID] 17-18, 26, 132

ICT Pty Ltd v. Sea Containers Ltd [Australia]...................................52 n. 10

In the Matter of an Arbitration between Builders Federal (Hong Kong) Limited and Joseph Gartner & Co. v. Turner (East Asia) Pte Ltd (1988) [Singapore] (Turner case)... 36-37

J&P Avax SA v. Tecnimont SPA (2009) [France]..............................64 n. 37

J&P Avax SA v. Tecnimont SPA (2012) [France].............................36 n. 1

Jivraj v. Hashwani [UK] 51

K/S Norjarl AS v. Hyundai Heavy Industries Co. Ltd. [UK].............68 n. 58, 123 n. 4

La Société Commercial Caribbean Niquel v. La Société Overseas Mining Investments Ltd [France] ....64 n. 27

LCIA reference number 81160 (29 August 2009) ....55 nn. 29 & 33

LCIA reference number 81224 (15 March 2010).................... 55 n. 29, 32 & 33

Linnett v. Halliwells [UK] ....58 n. 60

Methanex Corporation v. United States [UNCITRAL] 30, 113

Mond & Mond v. Dayan Rabbi Isaac Dov Berger [Australia] .... 56 n. 51, 61

Railroad Development Corporation v. Republic of Guatemala [ICSID] .... 114 n. 6
Ranger v. Great Western Railway Co. (1854) [UK] (Brunel case) 36

Shandong Hongri Acron Chemical JSC Ltd v. Petrochina International (HK) Corp. Ltd [Hong Kong] 126-127
SNF v. ICC [France] 121-122, 124, 126
Société Aranella v. Société Italo-Ecuadoriana [France] .... 72, 83 n. 21
Société Papillon Group Corporation v. Republique arabe de Syrie et al. [France] .... 82 n. 15
Soyak International Construction and Investment, Inc. v. Hober, Krause and Melis [Sweden] 123

The Loewen Group, Inc. and Raymond L. Loewen v. United States of America [ICSID] 113
The Rompetrol Group v. Romania [ICSID] 10, 17-18
Tidewater, Inc. and Others v. Venezuela [ICSID] 27-29

Universal Compression International Holdings, S.L.U. v. Bolivarian Republic of Venezuela [ICSID] .... 55 n. 35

ABOUT THE AUTHORS

DOAK BISHOP
PARTNER, KING & SPALDING, HOUSTON, UNITES STATES

Doak Bishop is Partner in King & Spalding's Houston office and Co-Chair of the firm's International Arbitration Practice Group. He holds a B.A. degree with high honours and departmental distinction from Southern Methodist University (1973), and a J.D. degree with honours from the University of Texas Law School (1976).

Mr Bishop has over 35 years of legal experience, with a focus on international arbitration and foreign investment disputes. He is member of the Board Certified in Civil Trial Law by the Texas Board of Legal Specialization, the Board of Directors of the American Arbitration Association, and the Board of Trustees of the Center for American and International Law. He is Vice-Chair of the Institute of Transnational Arbitration, a member of the U.S. delegation to the NAFTA Advisory Committee on Private Commercial Disputes, and advisor to the American Law Institute's Restatement of the Law (3rd) of International Commercial Arbitration. He was formerly Adjunct Professor, SMU Law School (1999) (International Commercial Arbitration) and University of Houston Law School (2002) (Foreign Investment Disputes), Co-Chair of the International Litigation Committee of ABA's Litigation Section (1998-2000) and Chair of the Litigation Section of the State Bar of Texas (1998-1999). He specializes in international arbitration, international energy disputes, investment and infrastructure disputes, construction disputes, and environment issues. He has registered more than 30 ICSID arbitrations and represented investors in about 40 investment arbitrations against foreign governments. He has been an arbitrator in about 70 arbitrations, including NAFTA and BIT arbitrations under the UNCITRAL Rules. He is editor of *The Art of Advocacy in International Arbitration* (2nd ed., Juris Publishing 2010), co-author with Professor James Crawford and Professor Michael Reisman of *Foreign Investment Disputes: Cases, Materials and Commentaries* (Kluwer, 2005), editor of Enforcement of Arbitral Awards Against Sovereigns (Juris 2009) and research editor of the *Texas Law Review.*

KARL-HEINZ BCKSTIEGEL
ARBITRATOR; CHAIRMAN, DIS, GERMANY;COUNCIL MEMBER, ICC INSTITUTE OF WORLD BUSINESS LAW

Karl-Heinz Böckstiegel was Chair of International Business Law and Director of the Institute of Air and Space Law, University of Cologne until 2001. He was President of the London Court of International Arbitration (LCIA) (1993-1997), Panel Chairman of the United Nations Compensation Commission (1994-1996), and President of the Iran-United States Claims Tribunal (1984-1988). Since 2001 he is an independent arbitrator and Professor Emeritus of the Law Faculty of the University of Cologne. Other functions include Chairman of the Board of the German Institution of Arbitration (DIS), Member of the ICC Commission on Arbitration, Patron of the Chartered Institute of Arbitrators and President of the International Law Association (ILA) (2004-2006).

Dr Böckstiegel has experience as party counsel, a mediator, an arbitrator and as president of the arbitration tribunal in many national and international arbitrations. He has authored 12 books and more than 300 articles and is the editor of 35 books.

TERESA Y.W. CHENG
SENIOR COUNSEL, DES VOEUX CHAMBERS, HONG KONG

Teresa Cheng GBS SC JP FICE FCIArb is a Senior Counsel, Chartered Engineer, Chartered Arbitrator and Accredited Mediator. She is Vice-President of the ICC International Court of Arbitration, appointed in 2009, as well as Vice-President of the International Council of Commercial Arbitration (ICCA) and Vice-Chairperson of the Hong Kong International Arbitration Centre (HKIAC). She is a member of the International Centre for Settlement of Investment Disputes (ICSID) Panel of Arbitrators, designated by the Chairman of the ICSID Administrative Council. She is a past President of the Chartered Institute of Arbitrators (CIArb) and a past Chairman of its East Asia Branch. She is also Council Member of the China International Economic and Trade Arbitration Committee (CIETAC), a member of the Asia Pacific Users' Council of the London Court of International Arbitration (LCIA) and a panel arbitrator of the Court of Arbitration for Sport (CAS). She also sits as a Deputy Judge in the Court of First Instance of the High Court of Hong Kong.

Ms Cheng is a Fellow of King's College, London, Visiting Professor at the School of Law of Tsinghua University, Beijing, and Adjunct Professor at the University of Hong Kong and Hong Kong Polytechnic University. She has co-authored numerous books and articles in journals and has presented papers at many seminars. Some of her recent publications include Construction Law and Practice in Hong Kong and Arbitration in Hong Kong: A Practical Guide, published by Sweet & Maxwell, as well as papers in the "International Council for Commercial Arbitration Congress Series", published by Kluwer Law International.

YVES DERAINS
FOUNDING PARTNER, DERAINS GHARAVI, FRANCE; FORMER SECRETARY GENERAL, ICC NTERNATIONAL COURT OF ARBITRATION; CHAIRMAN, ICC INSTITUTE OF WORLD BUSINESS LAW

Yves Derains, former Secretary General of the ICC International Court of Arbitration and Director of the Legal Department of the ICC, is a member of the Paris Bar and a Founding Partner of the law firm Derains & Gharavi. He is specialized in international arbitration and acts both as an arbitrator and counsel for parties in arbitration proceedings.

Mr Derains is a former Chairman of the Comité Français de l'Arbitrage and Chairman of the ICC Institute of World Business Law. He was Chairman of the Working Party on the Revision of the ICC Rules of Arbitration in 1998 and Co-Chairman of the ICC Task Force on the Reduction of Costs and Time in International Arbitration. He has been a member of the French Committee on Private International Law since 1978. He is member of the International Council for Commercial Arbitration (ICCA) and a member of various other organizations specialized in international arbitration and international business law. He is an Honorary Professor of the Law Faculties of San Ignacio de Loyola University and Universidad del Pacifico, Lima, Peru.

Mr Derains is also the author of many publications on International Commercial Arbitration and International Business Law, in particular: *Evaluation of damages in international arbitration* (ICC Institute of World Business Law, 2006) and *A Guide to the ICC Rules of Arbitration* (2nd ed., , with E. Schwartz) (Kluwer Law International, 2005).

JEAN-ANDRÉ DIAZ
SPECIAL COUNSEL, TOTAL E&P, FRANCE ; CHAIRMAN, CORPORATE COUNSEL INTERNATIONAL ARBITRATION GROUP

Jean-André Diaz is presently Senior Counsel at the Legal Department of TOTAL Exploration and Production.

As Legal Director, he has led a team of lawyers for many years and is personally in charge of negotiating and enforcing contracts for both the upstream and downstream sectors of the petroleum industry in many parts of the world (Africa, the Middle East, Northern and Central Europe and the Americas).

This has given him the opportunity to be regularly involved in international arbitrations under various rules and legal systems.

He is the Chair of the Oil and Gas Committee of the International Bar Association (IBA) and the Chair of the Corporate Counsel International Arbitration Group (CCIAG).

HAMID GHARAVI
FOUNDING PARTNER, DERAINS & GHARAVI, FRANCE

Hamid Gharavi, co-Founding Partner of the boutique arbitration firm Derains & Gharavi, is a member of the Paris and New York Bars.

He has acted as counsel and arbitrator in over 100 *ad hoc* and institutional commercial arbitrations as well as arbitrations under investment treaties.

Dr Gharavi is a Member of the LCIA Court and an appointee of the Kingdom of Cambodia to the ICSID Panel of Arbitrators.

He is the author of numerous publications on arbitration, including *The International Effectiveness of the Annulment of an Award* published by Kluwer.

JUDITH GILL, QC
PARTNER, ALLEN & OVERY LLP, UNITED KINGDOM

Judith Gill has been a Partner of Allen & Overy LLP since 1992. She graduated in Jurisprudence from Worcester College, Oxford University and in 1985 qualified with Allen & Overy as a solicitor. In 1990 she obtained a Diploma in International Commercial Arbitration, with distinction, from Queen Mary College, University of London and in 1998 qualified as a Solicitor Advocate (Higher Courts – Civil). She is only the second woman solicitor-advocate to be appointed QC and the first with an international arbitration practice. In July 2011 Judith won the award for "Best in Commercial Arbitration" at Euromoney's Women in Business Law Awards.

Ms Gill specializes in international commercial arbitration, with extensive experience in both institutional and *ad hoc* arbitration, including proceedings under the LCIA, ICC, ICSID, AAA and UNCITRAL rules, as well as many others. She is regularly appointed as an arbitrator and frequently appears as lead advocate in arbitration proceedings. Her arbitration practice covers a broad range of subjects including insurance, joint ventures, distributorships, projects and many other commercial dealings, and she has acted both for and against government entities.

Ms Gill holds appointments at many arbitral institutions and is currently Co-Chair of the Arbitration Committee of the International Bar Association Legal Practice Division, Vice-Chair of the International Commercial Dispute Resolution Committee of the ABA Section of International Law (ABA International), Director of the LCIA and former member of the LCIA Court, a Director of the SIAC, a Director of the AAA, Chair of the International Arbitration Club, Member of the ICC UK Arbitration Group, Fellow of the Chartered Institute of Arbitrators and a Fellow of the Institute of Advanced Legal Studies.

Ms Gill is joint author of the last three editions of the leading textbook Russell on Arbitration and has published widely on arbitration issues.

HORACIO A. GRIGERA NAÓN
INDEPENDENT INTERNATIONAL ARBITRATOR AND CONSULTANT, WASHINGTON D.C., UNITED STATES

Horacio Grigera Naón, presently an independent international arbitrator and consultant on arbitration, business and international law matters, is a former Secretary General of the ICC International Court of Arbitration and a practitioner in the field of international commercial arbitration and international business law for over 25 years.

As well as being a Distinguished Practitioner in Residence at the Washington College of Law, American University, Washington D.C. and the Director of the International Commercial Arbitration Center, he is also a member of the American Law Institute, a former Special Counsel with White & Case LLP and a former Senior Counsel with the International Finance Corporation, Washington D.C. He holds LL.M. and S.J.D degrees from Harvard Law School, LL.B and LL.D. degrees from the School of Law of the University of Buenos Aires and is a member of the Argentine Federal, New York, District of Columbia and United States Supreme Court Bars.

He has also published widely in these areas, including a book on *Choice-of-Law Problems in International Commercial Arbitration* (1992), and has lectured at the Hague Academy of International Law (2001).

BERNARD HANOTIAU
PARTNER AND PROFESSOR, HANOTIAU & VAN DEN BERG, BELGIUM; COUNCIL MEMBER, ICC INSTITUTE OF WORLD BUSINESS LAW; COUNCIL MEMBER, ICCA

Bernard Hanotiau is a member of the Brussels and Paris Bars. In 2001, he established a boutique law firm concentrating on international arbitration and litigation in Brussels. He is also a professor at the Law School of Louvain University where he teaches international arbitration. He has a PhD from Louvain University and an LL.M. from Columbia University (1973).

Since 1978, Mr Hanotiau has been actively involved in international commercial arbitration as a party-appointed arbitrator, chairman, sole arbitrator, counsel and expert in various parts of the world. He is a member of ICCA, the ICC International Arbitration Commission and a Council Member of the ICC Institute. He is also Vice-President of CEPANI and of the Institute of Transnational Arbitration (Dallas). He has written a major treatise on *complex arbitrations: Complex Arbitrations: Multiparty, Multicontract, Multi-issues and Class Actions* (Kluwer, 2006

KARL H. HENNESSEE
VICE-PRESIDENT, LITIGATION & REGULATORY AFFAIRS, AIRBUS SAS, FRANCE

Karl Hennessee is Vice-President and Head of Litigation & Regulatory Affairs at Airbus SAS in Toulouse, France, and with his team handles Airbus's litigation/contentious and legal regulatory matters. He also leads the EADS Group's Litigation Centre of Competence and lectures at the Toulouse Business School. Karl has previously practised law in Germany and in the United States on behalf of institutions including the German government's Federal Cartel Office, DaimlerChrysler, White & Case, Feddersen and Vinson & Elkins.

Educated at the University of Göttingen, Germany, the London School of Economics and SMU Law School, he holds degrees in history, economics and law (with a specialty in aviation). He is Vice-Chair of the ABA Aviation Litigation Section and a member of the Leadership of the ABA Antitrust Section, as well as a Fellow of the Robert Bosch Foundation and Phi Beta Kappa. Mr Hennessee was short-listed for the 2008 ILO Individual Litigation Award and was selected as the winner of the ILO Award for Litigation "Individual of the Year" for 2009. He has published over forty articles on various legal subjects and is currently a doctoral candidate in international comparative law at the Humboldt University (Berlin).

PETER LEAVER, QC
INTERNATIONAL COMMERCIAL ARBITRATOR, ONE ESSEX COURT, UNITED KINGDOM

Peter Leaver QC is an experienced international commercial arbitrator. Through his extensive practice at the Bar, Peter Leaver is experienced in banking, insurance and financial services and related jurisdictional issues. He is also experienced in sports cases. He was appointed to silk in 1987 and is Recorder of the Crown Court and a Deputy High Court Judge.

He is Chairman of the Board of the London Court of International Arbitration and sits in arbitrations in many parts of the world under the rules of many different institutions as well as arbitrations under the UNCITRAL Rules.

He was a member of the Court of Arbitration for Sport and was appointed as a member of the Ad Hoc Division of the Court of Arbitration for Sport for the Salt Lake City Olympic Winter Games 2002 and for the Turin Olympic Winter Games 2006. Between 1997 and 1999 he took a sabbatical from the Bar and was Chief Executive of the FA Premier League. He is currently the President of the United Kingdom National Anti-Doping Panel.

LAURENT LÉVY
PARTNER, LÉVY KAUFMANN-KOHLER, SWITZERLAND; VICE-CHAIRMAN, ICC INTERNATIONAL COURT OF ARBITRATION; COUNCIL MEMBER, ICC INSTITUTE OF WORLD BUSINESS LAW

Laurent Lévy, admitted to the Geneva Bar in 1974, has been a partner at Lévy Kaufmann-Kohler since 1 January 2008. Previously, he was a partner in the International Arbitration Department of Schellenberg Wittmer, Geneva and Zurich. He concentrates his activities on international arbitration. He is a Doctor at Law (Paris) and was educated at the Universities of Paris, Geneva and Wurzburg (Germany).

Dr Lévy is currently Vice-Chairman of the ICC International Court of Arbitration and Council Member of the ICC Institute of World Business Law. He is a former Vice-President of the LCIA Court (London). He is also Visiting Professor at the Centre for Commercial Law Studies, Queen Mary, University of London.

JULIAN D.M. LEW, QC
BARRISTER, 20 ESSEX STREET CHAMBERS, UNITED KINGDOM; PROFESSOR AND HEAD, SCHOOL OF INTERNATIONAL ARBITRATION, QUEEN MARY, UNIVERSITY OF LONDON; COUNCIL MEMBER, ICC INSTITUTE OF WORLD BUSINESS LAW

Julian Lew has been involved in International Arbitration for well over 30 years as both a practitioner and an academic. He has acted as chairman of arbitral tribunals, sole arbitrator and co-arbitrator under all the major international arbitration systems, including ICC, ICSID, LCIA, UNCITRAL, Swiss Rules and Stockholm Institute. Until 2005, he was a Partner at Herbert Smith and head of its International Arbitration Practice. He is Professor of Law and Head of the School of International Arbitration, Queen Mary, University of London. He has written and lectured extensively on all aspects of International Arbitration. He is a member of the ICC International Court of Arbitration (UK). He has an LL.B. from the University of London and a Doctorate in Private International Law from the Catholic University of Louvain.

JUSTIN LI

Justin Li graduated in 2012 with a Double-Degree (LLB/JD) from Columbia Law School and University College London with particular interest in investment law and in international commercial arbitration. During his time at Columbia, he was the senior editor of American Review of International Arbitration. During his studies, he has internships with Hogan Lovells (Hong Kong), Des Voeux Chambers (Hong Kong), Willem's Avocat (Paris) and Jones Day (Beijing). In summer 2011, he worked as a stagiaire for the International Arbitration Group at Freshfields Bruckhaus Deringer, Paris.

ANNETTE MAGNUSSON
SECRETARY GENERAL, ARBITRATION INSTITUTE OF THE STOCKHOLM CHAMBER OF COMMERCE, SWEDEN

Annette Magnusson is Secretary General of the Arbitration Institute of the Stockholm Chamber of Commerce (SCC), since 2010. She joined SCC from Mannheimer Swartling Advokatbyrå (Stockholm), where she was a member of the dispute resolution group. Before then she headed strategic planning of knowledge management at Baker McKenzie in Sweden. Mrs Magnusson was SCC Deputy Secretary General and SCC Legal Counsel from 1998 to 2005. She is the author or editor of several publications on international arbitration, a member of the Research Panel for Arbitration Law at the Stockholm Centre for Commercial Law, and a frequent lecturer.

ALEXIS MOURRE
PARTNER, CASTALDI MOURRE & PARTNERS, FRANCE;
VICE-PRESIDENT, ICC INTERNATIONAL COURT OF ARBITRATION;
VICE-CHAIRMAN, ICC INSTITUTE OF WORLD BUSINESS LAW

Alexis Mourre is a founding Partner of Castaldi Mourre & Partners, a 25-lawyer firm with offices in Paris and Milan. He heads the international arbitration and litigation department of the firm. As of September 2012, he has acted in more than 200 *ad hoc* or institutional commercial arbitration proceedings as counsel, expert witness, co-arbitrator, chairman or sole arbitrator.

His arbitration experience includes, in particular, mergers and acquisitions, shareholders' agreements, joint ventures, competition, investment disputes, telecommunications, air and space, construction and energy. He is author, co-author or editor of several books, including *Written Evidence and Discovery in International Arbitration* (ICC Publishing, 2009), *Droit judiciaire privé européen des affaires* (Bruylant, 2003), *Le nouveau droit communautaire de la concurrence* (Bruylant, 2004), and *Mondialisation, politique industrielle et droit communautaire de la concurrence* (Bruylant, 2006). He is founder and past director of the *Paris Journal of International Arbitration*, a leading French publication on arbitration and ADR. He lectures on arbitration in several universities and regularly intervenes as a speaker in seminars and congresses on international arbitration. He has published more than 80 articles on arbitration and private international law.

Alexis Mourre is Vice-President of the ICC International Court of Arbitration and Co-chair of the IBA Arbitration Committee. He is Vice-President of the ICC Institute of World Business Law, member of the court of the LCIA and member of the Arbitral Council of the Milan Chamber of Commerce. He is member of the ICC international arbitration commission as well as of the ILA arbitration commission. He is member of numerous associations, including the ASA, the LCIA, the Milan Club of arbitrators, and the Institute for Transnational Arbitration (Advisory Board).

Alexis is fluent in French, English, Spanish and Italian. He has a working knowledge of Portuguese.

CONSTANTINE PARTASIDES
PARTNER, DIRECTOR OF INTERNATIONAL ARBITRATION, FRESHFIELDS, BRUCKHAUS DERINGER LLP, FRANCE

After practising international arbitration at Freshfields' Paris office for ten years, Constantine Partasides has returned to head the Freshfields international arbitration group in London. He has acted as counsel and arbitrator in over 50 *ad hoc* and institutional arbitrations, including under the rules of UNCITRAL, ICC, LCIA, AAA and ICSID. He has appeared as counsel in some of the largest commercial arbitrations of the last decade in the energy, telecommunications and satellite sectors. He has also advised and represented a variety of investors and states in disputes under various bilateral and multilateral investment treaties. Mr Partasides is a co-author of the fourth and fifth editions of the leading textbook on international arbitration *Redfern and Hunter on International Arbitration*. He is a solicitor-advocate (Higher Courts – Civil).

EDUARDO SILVA ROMERO
PARTNER, DECHERT LLP, FRANCE; ASSOCIATE MEMBER, ICC INSTITUTE OF WORLD BUSINESS LAW

Eduardo Silva Romero specializes in litigation and arbitration matters, particularly international disputes involving state entities, as well as Spanish and Latin American parties.

An acknowledged expert in international arbitration, he has supervised numerous proceedings before arbitration panels worldwide. Former Deputy Counsel, Counsel and Deputy Secretary General of the ICC International Court of Arbitration, Mr Silva Romero's far-reaching experience includes international sales and distribution contracts, construction, oil, M&A and electricity-related disputes. He has advised or acted as an arbitrator on arbitration matters conducted under the auspices of ICC, ICSID, AAA and the Stockholm Chamber of Commerce, as well as in *ad hoc* proceedings under the UNCITRAL Arbitration Rules. Mr Silva Romero is the Chairman of the ICC Task Force on Arbitration involving States or State Entities. He joined Dechert LLP from Coudert Brothers' Paris office in 2005.

Recognized as one of the top 45 lawyers under the age of 45 (45 under 45) by *Global Arbitration Review*, Mr Silva Romero is also listed in the Legal 500, Chambers Europe, Chambers Latin America and Décideurs Stratégie Finance Droit.

He is admitted to the Colombian and French Bars, is fluent in Spanish, French and English and has a working knowledge of Portuguese.

MARGRETE STEVENS
CONSULTANT, KING & SPALDING, WASHINGTON D.C., UNITED STATES

Margrete Stevens joined King & Spalding's International Arbitration Group as a consultant in 2007, after working for nearly 20 years at the World Bank Group's International Centre for Settlement of Investment Disputes (ICSID), where she served as senior counsel. Ms Stevens serves as a Member of the Board of the Stockholm Chamber of Commerce Arbitration Institute and is the Founding Member of the Washington, D.C. International Arbitration Club. In addition, she is a former Vice-Chair of the International Bar Association's Mediation Committee and a member of the IBA Task Force on Counsel Ethics in International Arbitration. Ms Stevens holds a Cand. Jur. degree from the University of Copenhagen and an LL.M. from the London School of Economics.

PIERRE TERCIER
EMERITUS PROFESSOR, UNIVERSITY OF FRIBOURG, SWITZERLAND; HONORARY CHAIRMAN, ICC INTERNATIONAL COURT OF ARBITRATION

Pierre Tercier is former Chairman of the ICC International Court of Arbitration. A Swiss national and emeritus professor at the University of Fribourg, Switzerland, he has extensive international arbitration and dispute resolution experience, having served on numerous occasions in ICC, ICSID and other cases. He is highly respected in the international legal and business community as an arbitrator, lecturer and author. He formerly chaired the Swiss Antitrust Commission and the Swiss Insurance Law Society. He is visiting professor of law at numerous universities, including Geneva and Paris. He graduated from the University of Fribourg *summa cum laude* and was admitted to the bar in 1969. In 2004, he was awarded an Honorary Doctorate by the University of Paris II. He is member of the ASA Board and a Council member of the ICCA.

V. V. VEEDER, QC
ESSEX COURT CHAMBERS, UNITED KINGDOM; COUNCIL MEMBER, ICC INSTITUTE OF WORLD BUSINESS LAW

V. V. Veeder practises as an advocate and arbitrator, in London and abroad, specializing in commercial law and international trade, from Essex Court Chambers. He is also Visiting Professor for Investment Arbitration at King's College, University of London. He is a Council Member of ICCA and the ICC Institute of World Business Law. He is Vice-President and Member of the London Court of International Arbitration and was Chairman of LCIA Limited from1999 to 2003. He is a Member of the Contract Recognition Board for FIA Formula 1 World Championship (Geneva) and was Member of the TAF World Cup Division for 2002 FIFA World Cup Korea/Japan. He was Member of the United Kingdom's Department of Trade and Industry Advisory Committee on the Law of Arbitration from 1990 to 1996, and General Editor of *"Arbitration International"* from 1985 to 2006.

THE INTERNATIONAL CHAMBER OF COMMERCE

ICC is the world business organization, a representative body that speaks with authority on behalf of enterprises from all sectors in every part of the world.

The fundamental mission of ICC is to promote open international trade and investment and help business meet the challenges and opportunities of globalization. Its conviction that trade is a powerful force for peace and prosperity dates from the organization's origins early in the 20th century. The small group of far-sighted business leaders who founded ICC called themselves "the merchants of peace".

ICC has three main activities: rule setting, dispute resolution, and policy advocacy. Because its member companies and associations are themselves engaged in international business, ICC has unrivalled authority in making rules that govern the conduct of business across borders. Although these rules are voluntary, they are observed in countless thousands of transactions every day and have become part of the fabric of international trade.

ICC also provides essential services, foremost among them the ICC International Court of Arbitration, the world's leading arbitral institution. Another service is the World Chambers Federation, ICC's worldwide network of chambers of commerce, fostering interaction and exchange of chamber best practice. ICC also offers specialized training and seminars and is an industry-leading publisher of practical and educational reference tools for international business, banking and arbitration.

Business leaders and experts drawn from the ICC membership establish the business stance on broad issues of trade and investment policy as well as on vital technical and sectoral subjects. These include anti-corruption, banking, the digital economy, telecommunications, marketing ethics, environment and energy, competition policy and intellectual property, among others.

ICC works closely with the United Nations, the World Trade Organization and other intergovernmental forums, including the G20.

ICC was founded in 1919. Today it groups hundreds of thousands of member companies and associations from over 120 countries. National committees work with ICC members in their countries to address their concerns and convey to their governments the business views formulated by ICC.

SOME ICC SPECIALIZED DIVISIONS

- ICC International Court of Arbitration
- ICC International Centre for Expertise
- ICC World Chambers Federation
- ICC Institute of World Business Law
- ICC Centre for Maritime bureau
- ICC Commercial Crime Services
- ICC Services

- **Publications**

ICC Publications Department is committed to offering the best resources on business and trade for the international community.

The content of ICC publications is derived from the work of ICC commissions, institutions and individual international experts. The specialized list covers a range of topics including international banking, international trade reference and terms (Incoterms), law and arbitration, counterfeiting and fraud, model commercial contracts and environmental issues.

Publications are available in both traditional paper and electronic formats from the ICC Business Bookstore.

- **ICC Training and Conferences**

ICC's programme of conferences and seminars is the essential channel for passing on the world business organization's expertise to a wider audience.

ICC Training and Conferences, a Department of ICC Services, spotlights policy issues of direct concern to business such as banking techniques and practices, e-business, IT and telecoms, piracy and counterfeiting.

ICC Training and Conferences also runs training courses on international arbitration and negotiating international contracts for business people, corporate counsel, lawyers and legal practitioners involved in international trade.national committee in your country are available at www.iccwbo.org.

ICC PUBLICATIONS FOR GLOBAL BUSINESS

ICC's list of specialized publications covers a range of topics including international banking, international trade reference and rules (the Incoterms® rules), law and arbitration, counterfeiting and fraud, model commercial contracts and environmental issues.

ICC products are available from ICC national committees, which exist in over 90 countries around the world. Contact details for a national committee in your country are available at www.iccwbo.org

You may also order ICC products online from the ICC Business Bookstore at www.iccbooks.com, or purchase them at the ICC Secretariat, located at the address below.

ICC Publications
38 Cours Albert 1er
75008 Paris
France
Tel.   +33 1 49 53 29 23
Fax.   +33 1 49 53 29 02
e-mail   pub@iccwbo.org

International Chamber of Commerce
The world business organization

LATEST ARBITRATION PUBLICATIONS FROM ICC

Order now at www.iccbooks.com or fill in and return the order form on the back. Visit our online Bookstore for a complete list of publications.

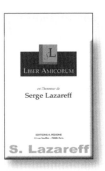

ORDER FORM

Order online at www.iccbooks.com or fill in and return this form by fax
(+33 (0)1 49 53 29 02), post (see below) or email (pub@iccwbo.org).

Pub. No.	Title	Price in € H.T without tax	Quantity	Total

Subtotal €..

Postage: add 20% for priority Airmail or 30% for Courier Service €..

EU customers without intra-community VAT number*: add 7% VAT €..

Total €..

[ ] Please tick here if you need a pro-forma invoice.

Payment Options: Please note that all orders must be prepaid.

[ ] Cheque
Payable to ICC Services

[ ] Bank Transfer (please send copy of bank transfer)
HSBC, 103 Av. des Champs Elysées, 75008 Paris, France
IBAN: FR76 3005 6007 2807 2836 8014 517
BIC: CCFRFRPP
For customers in France, RIB: 30056 00728 07283680145 17

[ ] Credit Card number...Expiry date ....
Company...Contact Person.......................................
Address...
City..............................Zip..........................Country.................Phone/Fax ....
Email...Sector of Activity..
Intra-Community VAT No.*..

Date....................................Signature............................

* EU customers are requested to provide their Intra-Community VAT Number without which 7% of the total order value will be added as VAT.

N.B. In accordance with the French Act on Data Processing, Data Files and Individual Liberties (Loi informatique et libertés) from 1978, you are free to access and change information you provide at any time. Simply email pub@iccwbo.org in order to change, update or correct your data.

ICC Services SAS
An affiliate of the International Chamber of Commerce (ICC)
38 Cours Albert 1er, 75008 Paris, France
Intra-community VAT number: FR 45 313 975 237
Customer service: Tel +33 (0)1 49 53 30 56/28 89, Fax +33 (0)1 49 53 29 02
E-mail: pub@iccwbo.org Website: www.iccbooks.com

ICC
International Chamber of Commerce
The world business organization